When the Martians Land in Huddersfield

When the Martians Land in Huddersfield

Mike Harding

ARROW BOOKS

For Rochelle

Arrow Books Limited
17-21 Conway Street, London W1P 6JD

An imprint of the Hutchinson Publishing Group

London Melbourne Sydney Auckland
Johannesburg and agencies throughout
the world

First published in Great Britain
by Robson Books Ltd 1984
Arrow edition 1985

Printed and bound in Great Britain
by Anchor Brendon Limited, Tiptree, Essex

ISBN 0 09 941710 3

Contents

ALL CARTOONS AND
LETTERING

BY MIKE HARDING.

Charles Dickens on a reading tour of the USA, reading from 'The Day The Sky Fell On Chuckey Luckey's Head'.

Dear God

Some years ago, I was working on the Christmas post and was sat in the canteen one night stuffing a rock-hard cheese and onion down the old yawn box when one of the lads came in with a letter addressed to God. In the absence of a forwarding address, and since none of us particularly thought we'd be seeing God face to face in the near future, we opened the envelope. Inside was the first of some ten letters that arrived over the next few weeks, stopping suddenly, seemingly without any reason, although rumours did go round that a shaven-headed 'Pete' had been seen in a yellow nightie and an anorak banging some finger cymbals together on the pavement outside Chelsea Girl and the Cut Above unisex hair salon.

Be that as it may, in the absence of anybody to give permission, here are the unexpurgated letters to God from Pete.

Dear God,

I have decided to write to you tonight after what happened when I was just speaking to you. I asked for three knocks on the ceiling for 'yes' and two for 'no', and instead there were thirty-seven followed by a pause and the noise of a record being put on of Leonard Cohen singing 'Suzanne Takes Me Walking', or whatever it's called, then another 126 fast knocks followed by complete silence, which makes me think it wasn't a signal from you at all but Reg in the flat above with another nurse he's brought home, 'to see his stamps' he calls it. I wish he'd oil his bed.

Come to think of it, I've been wondering if you've been getting a bit deaf recently, since quite a few of the things I asked you about didn't happen, or else happened funny.

Like when I changed the date of my holidays because you said 'Yes, the end of August in Cleethorpes would be sunnier than at the beginning', and it wasn't because, as you must know, it rained for the whole fortnight and we (that is me and Diane) were double-booked with that Icelandic couple that were over here for the Water Diviners' conference. Anyway, Diane went home after three days and said she wished she'd gone to the Elvis Convention in Shrewsbury with Darrell instead, so it looks as though things between me and Diane have taken a backward step. So I wonder if you really did hear me?

Because of that I've decided to write to you direct from now on. I don't know your address, but I expect the Post Office will redirect my letters, and I know you'll find some way of reading them when you get a quiet moment away from all them choirs and thrones and powers and dominations and all that.

So, to repeat the question I asked tonight: Is it worthwhile me getting the tickets for the speedway on Wednesday, or will Bill Torrence's leg still be playing him up? A bit of thunder on Monday would mean 'yes' and an earthquake in the Middle East 'no.

Cheers!

Your mate, *Pete*

PS The cat has not come back since Reg spilt the paint on him, but you probably know that.

PPS It was great news about Reagan and the neutron bomb. That should show the Communists that he means what he says. I'm glad you're on his side.

Dear God,

Eric showed me a bit of his one
thousand part encyclopaedia that
says all matter is composed of atoms
and molecules in constant motion.
Eric says if that's true then it's
no wonder he's got piles. I don't
really understand his reasoning, but
then again he's like that. What I
want to know is this - if all them
molecules are moving, why do things
like the table I'm writing on look
as though they aren't? I've watched
it for over half an hour and none of
it's moved. Puzzling really.

Cheers!

Your mate,

Pete

Dear God,

Erïc said he read somewhere that a bloke called Darwin discovered that we are not descended from Adam and Eve but come instead from monkeys. I said, 'Where's Darwin now?' He said, 'Dead.' I said, 'There you are then, a fat lot he knows about it!' It's not a valid argument really but it shut him up for a bit.

Pete

PS I must tell you what happened when you sent the lightning last week. We were all in the flat and Eric and Tracey were drinking and rolling a joint when the lightning hit the chimney-pot and fused all the lights. Eric got up and knocked all the dope onto the electric fire, which was still going. It was three days before any of us woke up, so we've given up dope now.

PPS I've got a job from the dole this morning, stacking cans in Sainsbury's, so I won't be able to write so much now.

Dear God,

A bloke at work asked me how it was
possible to be a practising
Christian in this day and age when
it's proved beyond doubt that all
matter is composed of molecules,
time is cyclical, etc. and other
confusing things. I know he was
trying to get me going so I just
said, 'It's all a matter of faith.
You've either got it or you
haven't.' He said, 'Like squinting
eyes or a hump back?' I said 'Yes'
and he laughed.

I'm not sure who won that argument —
are you?

Your mate,

Dear God,

I got up this morning to catch the sunset. And I must admit it was one of your better ones, although you went a bit over the top with the magenta. Your clouds are getting a lot better nowadays too, you really seem to have got the hang of those nimbus, and last night's sunset with the mackerel-shoaled sky was a bazzer. Any news yet about the end of the world? Only my insurance man wants me to buy some insurance and it seems a waste of time if I'm never going to collect it. I may as well buy that new fishing-rod with the money.

Cheers!

Your mate,

Pete

PS Eric says thanks for the hangover, but I think he's being sarcastic.

13

Dear God,

I had to laugh yesterday. Eric was
in one of his 'don't believe in God'
moods, and had just said, 'I don't
believe in a prime mover any more,
in fact I think I'm a Pankeist' when
we were tidying up the flat and a
drawer fell on his foot. He jumped
up and banged his head on a cupboard
door, and jerked out of the way,
smashing his nose on the table! It
bled all over those white cords he
used to wear to pull all the birds
in Ibiza....

He reeled round the flat and cracked
his shin on the Habitat table that was
lying on its side. He'd just hopped
across the room shouting 'Oh God, Oh
God!' when he knocked a pot of pickled
beetroot on the cat. The cat scorched
out of the flat just as the landlord
was coming in, and clawed its way
over the landlord's head pulling his
toupee off. The dog thought the toupee
was a rat and ripped it to pieces. I
was almost sick laughing. You
certainly rubbed it in with Eric this
time. The landlord's so mad he's put
his rent up and made him move his
motorbike out of the lobby.

Yours, in admiration,

Pete

Dear God,

We were sat outside the boozer (The Merry Programmer) the
other day, having a few beers and a Ploughman's and that,
when Eric got into a bit of a row with Malcolm about you. You
know Malcolm, he's that lapsed Catholic that was into Zen and
Leylines and magic mushrooms a bit back. Well, he's just had
what he calls a 'personality crisis' because his lady's
buggered off with her lecturer (you remember, she was doing a
course in Sociology for a degree to help her with her work in
the Women's Movement) and she's taken Jason with her. Anyway,
Malcolm was really down last Sunday dinner-time and was
knocking back the lunatic soup like there was no tomorrow,
and he started ranting on about what a bag of fundament the
world was and how if there was a God he was either a pillock
or a Sadist (Belsen, Aberfan, Biafra etc.) and just as he
was working himself up into a lather a bird walked past with
long blonde hair, tight jeans and the biggest pair of bosoms
you've ever seen with no bra and a thin T-shirt on. Old
Malcolm choked on a mouthful of pork scratchings and lager
and Eric had to slap his back a couple of times to help him
breathe. I just leaned over and said, 'God made them bosoms
as well as Belsen, y'know.' And he didn't say anything, just
got up and walked off with his eyes watering, but whether it
was what I'd said or the pork scratchings, I don't know.
Still, he left his lager, so me and Eric split it between us.

It's an ill wind, etc

Yours bemusedly,

Dear God,

I'm sorry my last letter sounded so complaining. I know you were born in a stable and still managed to make it, but not everybody has the good luck to have himself as his own father, if you see what I mean. Anyway, the spots have cleared up now, so I might be able to go out again soon. Eric wants to know why, if you know how everything's going to turn out (being as how you're omniscient), you bothered starting it all in the first place? I think that he's got a point there. Can you let me know what you think? He also wants to know why you invented piles, since he's suffering with them very badly and walks round a lot trying to sit down. Can you give him a sign or something, as he keeps walking in front of the TV screen during 'The Generation Game', whimpering and saying 'If only you knew, it's all right for you lot, etc.'

Cheers!

Dear God,

Eric says he read about a guy called
Nostradamus who says the world's
ending next year, so he's cashed all
his insurance and gone out to get
drunk and screwed wearing my best
sweater, and he's also cancelled his
subscription to that one thousand
part encyclopaedia. Can you give him
a sign that will stop him, otherwise
my sweater will get ruined?

Thanks,

Pete

PS It's all right now, he's just
come in with a split lip some bloke
gave him in a pub. Apparently the
bloke has a bit of a hump and when
Eric said, 'Let's all drink to
Nostradamus the bloke thought he'd
said, 'Let's all drink to Notre
Dame,' i.e. Eric was laughing at his
hump. So he hit him with an RNU
lifeboat full of coppers and split
his lip. Eric came in and said, 'A
hunchback hit me with a lifeboat,'
so I thought there's a sign if ever
there was one.

Cheers!

Pete

PPS My sweater's ruined.

Dear God,

The Post Office have been returning
some of your mail unopened. Have you
got a new address?

Cheers!

Pete

Norman refused to answer the scientologist's questions.

Scenario For A Northern Play

Imagine if you can that it is the year 2050 in any northern town. South of Birmingham, an electrified fence has been built to keep the ravaging northern hordes in their place. Gates in the fence allow the A1, M1 and M6 motorways to bear northwards armed convoys of chemical and nuclear waste which is to be buried in the contaminated wastelands of what the south now calls Endworld.

Below Birmingham rumours are rife concerning the mutants that can be found north of the wall: two-headed people, dogs with seven legs, birds with no wings, second-hand car-salesmen with warm blood, and other abominations. The truth is more boring. The north is now an archipelago of ravaged cities, their centres a cluster of empty concrete shells, the haunts of gangs of the terminally employed whose chief diet seems to consist entirely of micro-fish and chips with VAT. Outside the cities, the festering remains of garden centres with their peeling sub-Disneyworld facades and their riotous acres of weeds, mutated by the pools of chemical waste that underlie the tips on which they were built, are now the homes of the mad and tottering remnants of local government officials.

Millions are living buried up to their necks in a sea of strya-foam cups. Safari overland trips are arranged from the south of England so that zoom-lensed, their noses pressed on the tinted windows of heated luxury coaches, the cogniscenti of Saffron Walden and Chew Magna can trundle slowly past the acres of naked people crawling over the mountains of empty Coke cans, fried chicken boxes and discarded, knitted poodle toilet-roll holders.

Expectantly believing in the myth of the Man From Whitehall who is to come north, like a new cargo cult, bearing in his hands the future, bringing with him new solutions or promises of solutions or promises of promises of solutions, these people are forgotten, unwanted, an embarrassment to the government, bit-part actors in a play with a cast of millions, a new sub-Beckett drama called 'WAITING FOR GOBO'.

20

The Most Influential Woman in my Life

The most influential woman in my life was a girl that loomed large in my pubescent fantasies and who, for brevity's sake, I'll call Una - Una Tainable. It sounds French and sometimes she was. Una Tainable was the girl I always longed for, the girl that passed me by in a crowded room, the girl stood in front of me in the library or at the bus stop, the Una Tainable Una.

She was unattainable for a number of reasons. Sometimes she was travelling too fast and in the wrong direction, sometimes we were separated by the sock counter in Marks and Spencer and once, only once, she was a nun. A brief eye-to-eye contact and a flash - of what? Recognition? Puzzlement? Boredom? Incredulity? Who can tell? But those passing glimpses of the Unas in my life left scars on my psyche like Shermen tracks in mud.

One of the worst moments was meeting her on the 'down' escalator in a big department store in Manchester. I was fifteen years old, with a Billy Fury haircut, fly away ears and the collar on my school blazer turned up so that I looked like a cross between James Dean and Quasimodo.

This Una had thick red hair in two long plaits that went all the way down to the bottom of her blazer. Her skin was fair and freckled and her almond eyes as she looked at me burned into my inner being and stirred the murky waters of lust that bubbled in the cauldron of my soul.

She was with two friends. Two ugly, fat friends, with lank, ordinary brown hair, cut short, and twin galaxies of spots. One of them even had a brace on. They pointed at me and laughed. Una looked at me and smiled gently. I swooned, falling weak-kneed onto a bus conductor and a drunk with a bottle in a brown paper bag who were in front of me on the moving stairs.

Reaching the bottom of the escalator, I ran quickly to the 'up' stairs; they were crammed with women with big legs and string shopping-bags. Without a machine gun I couldn't get past them. I felt like Zhivago on the tram.

When I finally got to the top, Una and the two bears had disappeared. I searched the store for an hour. No luck. I was late home. My tea was cold. My mother moaned at me. No-one understood.

All I had of this particular Una was the memory and the fact that, not being totally stupid, I'd recognized the uniform. She was at The Hollies, a girls' Convent School not a million miles from the Catholic boys' school I went to where men with white collars back to front spent seven hours a day forcing facts into the grey matter of pubescent lumpy-faced boys with nothing but girls on their minds.

A month later, one of the lads in the form above announced that he was giving an all-night party. His folks were going away, poor, foolish mortals, leaving their semi in Chorlton to the mercy of twenty or so of Manchester's teenagers. I didn't expect to get an invite. I wasn't even in the running. The lad in question was a handsome, blonde, beefy, rugger-playing plank, destined for a career in Accountancy or the Law, four children, a detached house in the outer suburbs, a Ford Cortina GL, and life-time membership of the Rugby club.

21

I was one of what was known on the Rugby field as the 'odds and sods' or 'pick 'n' mix'. We were the weaklings, the conscientious objectors who could see no point at all in running round a muddy field in the rain, trying to carry a piece of leather between two sticks of a letter 'H', while big, beefy blokes tried to break bits of you off. Every games afternoon we'd stand shivering on the touch-line while the teams were picked; every shape and size from giraffe-like myopics with white, pimply thighs looking like bleached grasshoppers, to tubby circus midgets with faces like distorted cottage loaves.

I wore glasses. I'd played Rugby until I was fourteen when my failing eyesight got so bad I scored a home try in the face of no opposition and total amazement from my own team. I just couldn't see the direction I was supposed to be running in. I couldn't work out why there were no cheers. Poor Father Rigby, our coach, just shook his head on the touch-line and came the closest to swearing I ever heard him come. 'You feeb boy,' he said sadly, 'You feeb.'

So I didn't expect to be invited to the stars' party. I expected to be excluded along with all the swots, train spotters, acne kings, dandruff champions and crystal-set builders of the lower fifth.

But I had forgotten two things. Firstly, as the class idiot, I was generally good for a laugh if nothing else, and secondly, I played the guitar.

'Come to the party,' he said. 'Bring a bottle and your guitar. There's a lot of girls coming from The Hollies.'

The Hollies! The words did things to my body that I didn't think possible. 'Yes,' I said, my words as thick as yesterday's porridge.

Next Saturday, having spent all day shaving round the spots, washing my hair, cleaning my teeth, and tuning the guitar, I bought a bottle of cheap apricot wine and got the bus to the 'nice, quiet' end of town.

It was a mild spring evening, the gardens of Suburbia breathed a heady scent. I knocked, entered, and started playing the guitar in an empty room illuminated only by a tropical fish-tank, hoping to look sexy and moody and James Dean-like as the girls came in. They were late coming. I was getting hoarse and had run through my entire repertoire of Buddy Holly numbers fourteen times before they started to arrive.

As luck would have it, Una came. My goddess. My darling. I had dreamt all week about her and me alone on a desert island. Her and me walking hand in hand. I dreamt that I dived into a flood-swollen river to save her blind and crippled little brother. 'My hero. I'll love you forever,' she said.

She came in the darkened room. I took a swig from the cheap wine, curled my lip like Marty Wilde and started to sing 'Be Bop A Lulla'. The two bears joined her. My voice cracked a bit.

A tall, giraffe-like boy fell down drunk and hit his head on my knee, nearly shattering my kneecap. I ignored him and carried on singing. I finished, they clapped. I smiled at Una, took another swig of the cheap wine, then another. I turned my head so she would see me profiled against the green glow of the fish-tank and started singing 'He'll Have To Go'.

The two bears began to giggle. So did Una. In less than half a minute they were rolling round the hall, their paper nylon underskirts crackling like a bush fire, tears of hysteria causing cascades of mascara to smudge their way down their cheeks like lava on the flanks of Mount Etna.

22

I didn't know until afterwards that, seen in profile with the fish-tank behind me, I looked as though guppies were swimming out of my nose, and as I hit the words 'the way I used to do' an angel fish swam in and out of my mouth.

That was bad. But worse was to come. Una went upstairs with the host not long after, to see the rugger cap he got for Lancashire boys, and never came down. I got atrociously drunk on the cheap wine, blundered into his room by accident (I swear) and found them doing very un-Catholic things to each other.

I staggered off down the landing and stairs which had suddenly become rubbery, and drank a bottle of port I found in a dusty cupboard. With the house moving around me, like the whale's belly round Jonah, I staggered into the dark room with the record player and the snogging couples. At one time I remember kissing one of the bears and ending up with a brace on the end of my tongue. Later still, I remember standing in the garden as the dawn chorus began, with seven other young bloods offering my dinner to the rhododendron bushes.

Since then Una has haunted my life in various guises, always with other men coming out of expensive restaurants, looking at pink things in Marks and Spencer, on escalators, retreating in one of my dreams, always smiling, always beautiful, always Una Tainable.

And maybe that's the way it should be. Perhaps if I ever get to talk to her she'll turn out to be the third bear.

Eamonn Andrews, disguised as the Virgin Mary, finds yet another unsuspecting victim for 'This Is Your Life'.

When the Martians Land in Huddersfield

When the Martians land in Huddersfield,
I'll tell you what we'll do,
We'll grab the little green buggers
And show 'em a thing or two.
Do they think they can come here, pinchin'
Our women and our jobs?
We'll make 'em work on the buses
With the rest of the bloomin' Frogs.
That's what we'll do, that's what we'll do.

Captain's log, stardate 20098. The Martians' space-craft, Gatkis, left Mars this morning en route for the planet Earth. Our mission to boldly go where no five-legged, three-eyed creatures had been before except Yates' Wine Lodge, Manchester.

The crew: myself, Captain Kak, Doctor Shmuck, Spotty, Corporal Ahooya Hooya, Sergeant Itchinakas, and Lieutenant Hitachi - God bless you!

According to the ship's computer, Earth is the third planet in the Solar System. Life-forms: animal and vegetable and draught Bass. The dominant life-form is a biped mammal called Man, composed mainly of wind and water. Man reproduces by taking his outer skin off and jumping up and down shouting, 'Fork!'

When the Martians land in Huddersfield,
I'll tell you what we'll do,
We'll grab the little green buggers
And give 'em some British food -
Plastic Wimpys, frozen chips,
And a pint of Watney's beer.
Three weeks of that, they'll feel so bad,
They'll bugger off home, no fear.
That's what they'll do, that's what they'll do.

Captain's log, stardate 20099, change hands. There was trouble at breakfast-time this morning when Doctor Shmuck ate one of Corporal Ahooya Hooya's eggs. The Corporal was very upset because she'd only just laid it. According to the ship's computer, the planet Earth is ruled by older members of the species with ulcers, piles and fading memories. We Martians find it strange that people so near the end of their lives should be allowed to cock it up for all those who come after them.

The people of the planet Earth also worship a dull, yellow metal called gold. Gold is found buried deep in the bowels of the earth. Poor men spend all their lives digging it up to give it to rich men, who then bury it back in bank vaults deep in the bowels of the earth. Something nobody seems to find strange.

Some people on Earth are kept locked up for long periods of time without food or drink and are shaken about in extremes of cold and heat unmercifully. This is called British Rail.

When the Martians land in Huddersfield
I'll tell you what we'll do,
We'll give them all the rotten jobs
Like cleaning out the loos.
Once you let a couple in,
The rest'll be here right nippy,
Before you know what's happened
We'll be covered with Martian chippys.
That's what they'll do, that's what they'll do.

According to universal records in God's library, the spacecraft, Gatkis, made planetfall in a place called England, a small island in the cold northern hemisphere of the planet, once a powerful nation, now sublet to American, Japanese and Arab interests.

It landed at a place called Manchester, at a place called Old Trafford, on a Saturday afternoon where at that moment a friendly match was taking place between Manchester United and Glasgow Celtic. Due to a lack of foresight on the part of the engineers, the spacecraft was the exact shape, size, colour and dimensions as a can of McEwan's Export, India Pale Ale.

A drunken Manchester United supporter saw the spacecraft land, picked it up, pulled off the control tower and the energizer ring, and drank the entire contents. Just before he died he turned to his friend and said: 'It tastes just like Martian's pee!'

When the Martians land in Huddersfield,
I'll tell you what we'll do,
We'll grab the little green buggers
And show 'em a thing or two.
Do they think they can come here, pinchin'
Our women and our jobs?
We'll make 'em work on the buses
With the rest of the bloomin' Frogs.
That's what we'll do, that's what we'll do.

Are you frightened of golliwogs?
Mentally unstable?
Possibly psychotic?
Were you beaten a lot when you were small?
Would you like to get your own back?
We're looking for people who can sing 'Land of Hope and Glory' and kick Chinamen at the same time.
Join the National Front!

26

We said "Frankincense" you cloth eared wazzock!!!

They've gone to Greenham Common!!

The Rhinoceros' Chair

PART ONE:
WHAT HAPPENED WHEN REGINALD WOKE UP

Gregor Kropotkin, a wood-louse usually domiciled under the bark of a lightning-felled oak tree in the Smerkenst Forest in the Yaraslov district of Czechoslovakia, awoke one morning to discover that during the night he'd been turned into a bank manager in Basildon. It was a traumatic awakening and one made more traumatic by the discovery that at his side, snoring gently, her cheeks rising and falling like the throats of a pair of rutting bullfrogs, her breath redolent of an unclean cow shed in a heat wave, was the biggest and fattest woman Gregor Kropotkin had ever seen.

Kropotkin's memories, which were later to form the basis of his minimalist novel, *Letters Under The Skin*, had hitherto been confined to his adventures (repetitive by nature and limited in their variety by the physical parameters of his universe) amidst the moist corrosions and the detritus of the vegetable world of the Smerkenst Forest. His reaction, at finding himself now inside the body of a balding Basildon banker, was one of raw panic. I must add that his panic would have been much less had he known that at that moment Reginald Farrar, one-time manager of the National Westminster Bank's Basildon branch, had simultaneously found himself in the body of a Czechoslovakian wood-louse and was in the process of dying, his death being brought about by the unthinkingly cruel beak of a thrush called Sasha who was totally oblivious of the effect of her actions on the world of metaphysics, the laws of probability, or the banking system of Basildon.

However, unaware as he was of this consoling fact, fear and regret clutched Gregor's heart like the fingers of a double-glazing salesman round a fat contract.

'What of Krensky?' he thought, his friend Krensky who he met each day by the horse-mushroom. Krensky the wire-worm, so good, so wise, so practised in the art of conversation; Krensky who had made the forest insects shudder with delight by his declaration, 'All is the Witness to the totality of The One' and, 'If sound is the setting in motion of waves through the air and, however much they diminish, those waves still carry on, then were our ears sensitive enough we would be able to hear the great feet of Hannibal's elephants cracking the crust of the snow in an Alpine Pass, the titters of delight of Madame de Mountespan as she pleasured herself in Louis XIV's bed, and Caesar crying 'Ouch! O Larks! Crikey! Yaroo! You rotters!' as the knife sank between his shoulder-blades.'

Kropotkin thought of Krensky and wept a little. Beside him, his wife belched loudly. Noises about the house told him other people stirred.

What was he to do?

How was he to manage?

He knew nothing at all of banking, nothing of life in Basildon. He only knew he was a bank manager because some inner voice, confused and scrambled and mixed with his own wood-louse squeak, told him so. He as yet knew hardly anything of the language these people spoke. Shadowy impressions flickered across his mind, memories yet latent in his new body. A Tiger Tim annual, a walk through the Cheddar Gorge with the Guildford branch of the Methodist Holiday Fellowship in 1938, a copy of *Health and Efficiency* smuggled inside the *Eagle* comic between 'Dan Dare' and 'Harris Tweed', showing poor muggy photographs of goose-pimpled people in Epping Forest, the men with beach balls held in front of them, the women with shiny white patches between their legs, monuments to the retoucher's art: all these images flickered through his mind like cabbages falling down a flight of stairs.

What was he to do?

How was he to manage?

The words 'peccadillo', 'merange' and 'praxis' came into his mind, followed by the image of an archbishop on fire. What was he to do?

He could distinguish at a taste between seventy-six different varieties of tree. He could tell the age of an oak or beech by its smell alone, and his tiny feet could feel the heart of a mole beating a metre below the earth's surface. He was superbly equipped for living below the bark of dead rotting trees. Now all he could feel was the weighty presence of this massive female, the slap of her breath like something dead and reduced to slime that Kropotkin had once stumbled into under an old elm, and the sudden crushing blow from her thigh as she flung it across his legs.

Kropotkin felt something stirring at the base of, what he knew, had he been a wasp, would have been called his abdomen. One of his legs, the small one between the two larger ones at the base of his shell, was starting to stiffen. 'I must be growing another leg,' thought Kropotkin. 'Strange, and yet what a warm, pleasurable sensation there is accompanying it. If it feels this good,' he thought, 'I should like to grow a thousand legs like Kafka the millepede. Then how happy I should be.'

What happened next I shall not describe in detail. Let it be enough to say that Kropotkin felt nauseous for several minutes afterwards, nauseous and yet strangely exhilarated, a contradiction of emotions he found difficult to resolve. Immediately after the event, which I will not talk about but which involved Kropotkin's wife and his third leg, Kropotkin's wife rose from the bed like an eruption in a lard-works and moved across the room in an avalanche of cellulite and brushed-nylon, stopping suddenly before the dressing-table. There, parts of her flanks and stomach remained in motion long after her heels were firmly planted in the mules with their bright pink, nylon-fur coronas.

'If I'm to come out of this madness alive,' thought Gregor/Reginald, 'I must watch very carefully the actions of this big thing.'

She reached down and placing her feet carefully, she pulled over her knees and thighs an arrangement of woven nylon and polythene rods that took masses of this white flesh and moved it to other areas so that her top half stuck out and her bottom half was compressed in. At this moment she reminded Gregor slightly of a deformed bumble bee. She then pulled on two sheer, gossamer tubes and fastened them to the nylon affair, pulled over herself a bigger tube with pictures of things that Gregor recognized as mimosas roughly printed on it and shuffled from the room calling out, 'Don't be long, Reginald, you've a very full day ahead of you.'

Gregor waited until her vast form had moved through the door, blocking out the morning light for a moment, the way an engine does when entering a tunnel. He looked about him wildly.

What was he to do?

How was he to manage?

Vague memories of his own and of Mr Reginald Farrar's struggled in his mind for domination. In the end neither won, and in a state of confusion nearing delirium, he staggered across the room towards the wardrobe.

PART TWO:
WHAT HAPPENED IN THE KITCHEN

Downstairs, gathering round the breakfast bar in the kitchen, the two younger Farrars were girding their loins and preparing to meet the day. Tracey, a girl of nineteen, had pulled her luminous-green and candy-pink hair into something resembling an African sunset, the nest of a bird on drugs, and a sea anemone that had eaten a variety of coloured things and had made itself ill. Her black lipstick served to emphasize the fish-belly pallor of a face in which a pair of eyes, rimmed with purple, looked like Saint Bernard paw-prints in a snowdrift. She wore a dress, tube-shaped, if shape it could be called, of which the pink slashes on the purple acrylic cloth perfectly matched the pink shoes with the purple laces. Looking at her would have produced catalepsy in the average schizophrenic.

Her brother Wayne, a year older, had a crop of boils that made his face look like a row of accordion buttons while his ears could have modelled for a turnstile. His hair-style gave his head the image of having been sawn in two by a circular saw which was still stuck in there, and his leather jacket was emblazoned with a swastika and the legends 'Heavy Metal', 'Kiss', 'Suck', 'Tarzan's Milkmen', 'The Ghouls' and 'Be Cruel to Nuns!'

Both children were eating bowls of Yummy Nosh Brek, making noises as they masticated that reminded Gregor of an army of plumbers trying to unblock an eternity of sinks. Their mother was humming tunelessly to herself while making the coffee, sounding like a sub-station on breakdown, and at the side of the fridge-freezer a very ancient poodle with carious teeth was licking its balls.

Into this scene of suburban idyll walked Mr Reginald Farrar, wearing one of his wife's blouses and underneath nothing but a pair of her knickers, one of her corsets and a pair of dark charcoal stockings.

'Good morning,' he said.

There was an hiatus. Gregor sensed in a flash that he had done something wrong, but knew immediately that, whatever happened, he had to survive. What he didn't know was that his predecessor in this body, now sadly deceased having provided elevenses for six fledgeling thrushes, had been bullied by his wife and children into becoming a weak, cringing little pustule of a man, whose voice rarely rose above a mutter. Now Gregor sensed an attack about to begin. His fighting wood-louse instinct surfaced within him like froth on a whirlpool.

Wayne pointed towards him and began to snort, the ring and chain that stretched from his nose to his ear rattling like a pocketful of loose change.

Gregor lunged across the table and grabbing him by the lapels, butted his son on the nose. He poured a bowl of Yummy Nosh Brek and milk over his daughter's head and, picking the poodle up by the tail, hit his wife on the head with it shouting loudly:

'May not a man dress as he wishes in his own home!'

His family fled the house: Wayne, his nose bleeding, Tracey, her hair a swamp of Dayglo and Yummy Nosh, his wife choking on poodle fur. All three were crying. He threw the dog after them. It picked itself up and in a state of confusion bit a stone, breaking its remaining teeth.

Gregor wandered back into the lounge with its paintings of charging elephants on the chimney breast, its shag-pile rug and log-effect fire, its vinyl-covered bar, Rotarian plaques and its G-Plan sofa. Something in a corner of the room caught his attention. On a teak sideboard, circa 1968 Swedish design, with a stainless steel candlestick, a wooden fruit-bowl carved in the shape of a diseased kidney, and a thick glass fish that nobody had ever found a use for - a present from his sister in Surbiton - was a picture of him and the fat woman thirty years before. The fat woman had a white tube on, he had a close-fitting thing like a shell wrapped round his body and his upper legs. He went upstairs and in a big teak-veneered box with doors that stood against the wall, he found an identical shell. With the picture off the sideboard to guide him held in his hand, he dressed carefully.

Survive, he told himself. You must survive whatever happens. A voice in his brain said, 'Drive to the bank.'

He went downstairs. There were keys hanging on a hook on the wall. He took them down and went out of the house. His brain, or perhaps more correctly Reginald's memory, working in fits and starts now, in the manner of a lawnmower on a frosty morning, took him to a low wooden hut attached to the side of the house. He opened the door. Inside was a shiny metal thing with words which his brain told him said 'Volvo 264 GLE'. He got into the metal thing through another door. He put one of the keys in a hole on a pole that had a round thing on it and turned the key. He heard thunder. The brain told him, 'Hurry, you'll be late. You've never been late in twenty-five years. Put it into drive.'

He looked at a stick by his hand with P, D, R, N, 1 and 2 on it. He put his foot down on a metal thing on the floor. The

thing roared. Every time he pressed his foot down there was more thunder. Gregor liked that. He put his foot right down to the floor and pushed the stick into D.

At that moment his wife and children, enlisting the help of a neighbour, Mr Swithin, who was in a bulb and wine club with Mr Farrar, were returning home to calm their husband, father and friend. Imagine their astonishment then when Mr Farrar, dressed in his wife's Crimpolene, salmon-pink trouser-suit, shot through the back wall of the garage in the family Volvo, demolishing the wooden garage and every garden gnome in sight.

With an expressionless face he struggled with the wheel, turning the car in a broadside across the lawn, ripping up the turf and destroying the bird-bath, the swing-seat and the concrete cherub that peed into the plastic Alpine pool, in one sweep before directing the car out towards the avenue.

Before they could escape he'd crushed Wayne's foot, knocked down Tracey and had catapulted his wife and Mr Swithin into the air. Arm in arm, describing a perfect arc, they free-fell into the water garden, smashing the windmill with the little windy man and ejecting the goldfish into the aubretia.

Luckily no-one was killed.

'Reginald,' sobbed the fat woman, spitting out chickweed.

'He's mad,' said Mr Swithin, pulling nervously at his noustache, inadvertently ripping his lip off.

PART THREE:
REGINALD'S TRIP TO THE BANK

Reginald's trip to the bank was not without its little traumas. He drove the wrong way down a dual carriageway, causing a Juggernaut full of eggs to overturn, covering the road with 25,000 broken eggs. A Danish bacon lorry, swerving to avoid the Volvo, hit a Reliant Robin which exploded in a shower of fibreglass. The bacon lorry skidded to a halt, its doors flew open scattering its load and as its driver escaped, the diesel tank exploded and the lorry and surrounding road became a holocaust of flames.

Luckily no-one was killed, but within minutes the road was covered with frying smokey best-back streaky bacon and devilled eggs, the aroma of which was spread rapidly by the breeze through the crisp morning air attracting tramps from miles around, adding to the confusion. The Volvo trundled on at 105 miles an hour towards Basildon town centre, ignoring traffic lights, driving directly across roundabouts and traffic islands, and only coming to a halt when, swerving to avoid an office-block, Reginald hit and derailed a goods train on the main line to London, ramming the Volvo inextricably into a wagonload of bananas.

Luckily no-one was hurt.

Abandoning his car, he walked the last two miles to the bank. Above him, the depressingly featureless concrete towers of Basildon town centre loomed threateningly, a monument to the New Brutalist School of Architecture and living proof that it is still possible to qualify as an architect after a full frontal lobotomy.

On the streets of Basildon, people moved aimlessly, flowing in the random patterns of Brownian motion, for all the world like ants in the hill next to Gregor's log in the forest. Empty-eyed and hopeless, they filed into the massive office-blocks like pennies going into a slot machine. Reginald opened the back door. What was he to do here? He couldn't remember. Gregor didn't know.

'Good morning, Mr Farrar, is everything all right?' A simpering young man approached him wringing his hands. This was Mr Gibson, the assistant bank manager, an evil-smelling, little runt of a man with acne so bad he looked as though he'd been carved out of pink strya-foam. Reginald hit him and carried on, leaving him senseless on the floor.

He walked into his office and found his secretary sitting at her desk. She put down her nail-file as he entered and pointed at the switching unit on her desk.

'Mr Williams is on the phone.'

'Who is Mr Williams?'

'Mr Williams?'

'Yes, who is Mr Williams?'

'He's the area manager, sir!'

'Give me the phone.' He took the phone.

'Williams, you're a little turd, an officious pile of middle-class, Masonic cak.' He put the phone down.

His secretary looked at him. He looked back at his secretary and without breaking his gaze, tore his desk diary in two.

'Are you all right, Mr Farrar?'

'How would you like me to stretch you over the desk and give you a right seeing too?'

His secretary backed out of the room, goldfish-mouthed and panda-eyed.

Mr Farrar walked into the bank. There were twenty or thirty people queuing at the counter. Farrar walked towards the tellers.

'Get off your chairs.'

The tellers backed off in amazement.

Reginald Farrar took handfuls of money from the drawers. Fives, tens and twenties, bound in hundreds and thousands by paper bands.

'Would you like some money?' he asked the open-mouthed customers.

There was a chorus of 'Too bloody true!' 'No problem!' 'Are you joking?' 'Chuck it over here!'

'Well, I am the bank manager, am I not?' he addressed Miss Elizabeth Smythe, one of the tellers, who with her large bust and engagement ring, was the archetype of lady bank-tellers everywhere.

She nodded speechless.

'Here you are then.'

And he flung money over the glass partition until every drawer was empty, and the floor was a scrum of walking sticks, shopping bags, hearing aids, boots, high-heeled shoes and flying fists.

The police came too late to save the money: the beneficiaries had fled the scene and were nowhere to be found. A crowd had gathered outside the bank. Some said there was a robbery, some said that there was a madman inside, one old lady said that Christ had come down to earth again. The crowd laughed at her, but she had twenty thousand pounds in her shopping bag.

At the police station, where they took him after a struggle, and in which he bit on the bottom two of the policemen who had tried to restrain him, Reginald was placed in a cell which was bare but for a bench, a lavatory pan, and a wooden chair and table. There his tie and shoe-laces were taken off him. Disconsolate, Gregor sat in his salmon-pink, Crimpolene suit, staring at the floor. He wished, oh how he wished he was back in the forest under the bark of his damp log. Life there had been beautiful in its simplicity. How he missed it.

A constable looked in two hours later through the peep-hole, and immediately raced round to the crime-desk.

'Incident to report, Sergeant.'

'What's happened, Constable?'

The constable, still shocked, blurted out: 'The prisoner has ate the table, Sir.'

NEXT WEEK: GREGOR MEETS THE QUEEN AND THE PRIME MINISTER - AND CAN'T TELL THE DIFFERENCE!

Do you have trouble remembering your name?
Do you like sitting on committees?
Can you drink gallons of tea?
Do you own, or could you borrow, a beard?
Would you find it impossible to organize a piss-up in a brewery?
The Labour Party thinks it might need you - possibly - if you're not too left wing. (We'll let you know. We'll put it up to the committee.)

* * * * * *

Do you like digestive biscuits?
Do you listen to James Last?
Do you feel confused, without hope?
Do you feel lost, unsure?
Do you feel that life is a swimming pool and you have a hole in your water-wings?
Join the SDP!

What happened when Mrs Sony dropped the first Walkman on the way to the patent office.

Every morning Robert amused the boss's daughter by farting 'The Bluebells of Scotland'.

THE COLLECTED PAPERS OF THE WILLIAM SMALL SMALL ORCHESTRA SOCIETY

These papers, previously thought lost forever, were discovered accidentally by two schoolboys in a wood in Essex. They were actually looking for bodies and had been hoping for at least a headless woman or a couple of dismembered gangsters, since their friends at the local comprehensive had discovered hundreds of such over the years. Imagine their surprise, however, when what lay inside the heavy, tarred canvas sack was no millionaire's wife à la Boleyn or antique dealer in a blue circle jumpsuit but, as one of them said at the time, 'Snuffink, ony a load of old papers and photers.'

His friend, however, was slightly more intelligent, and had recently, although only thirteen, learnt how to vandalize his own phone boxes. He had gone solo twice that week and made sixteen Telecom cubicles black holes in the Edison Bell galaxy.

He stratched his velvet-cropped head. 'Cud be worf summink. Der wos a fing on der telly wonst abaht a geezer wot fahnd a boowk.'

'Boowk! Boowk!' his friend shrieked, 'Wossa neffin wosname erm boowk gorra doo wivit?'

''m telenyer, ineye? De effin wosname boowk wot dis geezer fahnd wuz valerbul. Tuk it to a wosname museum. Wosname geezer givim fahsandser pahnds, dinee?'

'Fahsandser pahnds?'

'Yer, fahsandser pahnds! Sam boowks is valerbul, speshlly wosnames oldtype boowks, narmeen?' he said, leaping about like a man on a trampoline with St Vitus' dance.

So it was that the William Small papers came first into the hands of Johnny 'the Knowledge' Bristow, BA Strangeways, Walton and Hull, now working as a commodities broker on the London market, i.e. a fence.

He gave the lads a fiver for the massive bundle of papers and resold them for ten thousand pounds the same day to a London dealer in antique maps and documents who took them a week later to Sotheby's where they went under the hammer to the nation for five hundred thousand pounds, escaping a life time in the University of Texas library by a mere ten grand.

The papers were moved to the British Museum where, after much research and cataloguing, they now lie. The following is a condensed version of the official life of William Small, culled from the fragments of diaries and notebooks of a man who is arguably one of the greatest, if one of the most enigmatic, figures in British popular classical music.

WILLIAM SMALL - THE LIFE AND TIMES OF A MAN OF MUSIC

William Small was born on 23 September 1806, the youngest and middle child of seventeen children born to Ariadne and Mountjoy Small, pearl-fishers of Tettenhall, Staffordshire. Little is known about the Small family save that they were so poor that the only family photo of them still in existence was hand-drawn (see plate 1). It would appear that Mountjoy Small did not always walk on the correct side of the law since the Tettenhall Court records show that a certain Mountjoy Small was apprehended one night by a constable in one of Lord Stafford's fields with a ferret down his trousers. On being told that the defendant had seventeen children, the magistrate directed that the ferret be left down his trousers.

(Plate 1)

The only other time that the family are mentioned in legal documents is in 1813 when, during the annual tradition of 'The Passing Of The Beef' in which Lord Stafford passed through the village preceded by a slice of roast beef that was dangled above the dribbling jowls of the crowd, four of the Smalls were discovered to be tugging at artificial forelocks. They were tried, found guilty, pilloried, burnt through the gristle of the nose and sentenced to ten years shredding Weetabix.

They were so poor that William Small tells in his diaries how as a child he and his elder brother Zoroaster would stand outside the kitchen cellar gratings of the rich, chewing the steam as it rolled up between the bars.

'Zoroaster was adept at knowing which gratings produced the best steam. We would begin with soup at No. 17, progress to fish at 21, run back for our meat dish to no. 15, dash across for our vegetables to 14 and finish with dessert at 76.'

Zoroaster was killed by a knife grinder's cart one evening while running for toad-in-the-hole (which we are told is better than frog-in-the-throat).

At the age of four, like his brothers and sisters before him, William was sent to Dame Trotter's School to be taught mumbling and hedge-lurking, two Staffordshire crafts. It was at Dame Trotter's School that William's twin talents for music and blind-man's buff were first discovered, when during a game of blind-man's buff he picked up the school cat, placed it under his arm and played it like a set of bag-pipes.

'I remembered playing faultlessly the first fourteen bars of "Stabat Mater,"' he tells us in his diary, *'and I still have the scars to prove it.'*

His father, seeing his youngest child's propensity for music, bought him in his fifth year a pianoforte, which the poor boy spent three months trying to blow. A piano teacher was waylaid on the Wolverhampton road one night and persuaded with the aid of a sock full of wet sand to teach William the rudiments of piano playing. Each time William made a mistake the piano teacher was hit, a novel innovation in teaching theory.

'I can still see the blood on the keys and hear the whimpering of that poor fellow in my ears.'

After a month the teacher, who was convinced by now that he was a sun-dial, was released a gibbering loon and was later transported to the colonies for being an hour slow. William by now could play by ear 'Oft In The Stilly Night', which was incredible as it hadn't been composed yet. The years from his fifth year up to his fourteenth birthday, when he ran away to sea, are shrouded in mystery, his diary for those years contains simply one entry covering more than nine years. And across the pages in shaky handwriting is scrawled, 'Very boring with rude bits'. It is to be expected, however, that he would have been acquainted with the traditional Staffordshire pastimes of catching scurvy and beggary.

When William Small was fourteen years old his father hoisted the pianoforte onto his mother's back, gave her a pair of wheels to hold, and turning her face-down trundled her into Stafford where he sold the piano and his wife for money for drink. William fell to the floor in a swoon, took four grains of laudanum and ran away to sea. At first he ran inland and stowed away on a tram plying between Barnsley and Wakefield. There he was discovered hiding under the stairs and was ejected as a stowaway, catching his top lip in the tram-lines as he hit the ground, which necessitated him growing a moustache as soon as he could to cover the scar.

Retracing his footsteps, he made for Liverpool. He walked by night and slept under hedges by day, which meant that when he arrived in the city he was two inches shorter, was corpse white and had bark beetle. It was in Canning Street, Liverpool, while staggering out of 'Maggie May's Good-Time Piano Bar and Clinic' one Friday evening that William Small met Pink Dog, a cutlass-scarred seaman and window dresser, who got him a place on a four-masted schooner bound out for the west. From a surviving fragment of his diary we know that the captain of the *Albatross*, the boat that he slipped aboard, plying between Liverpool and the West Indies for rum, concertinas and nancy boys, was Captain Ezekial Robinson, a cruel and unrelenting man(see Plate 2).

(Plate 2)

Captain Robinson made William 'Shanty Boy' on learning of his musical ability.

'I had to shout incomprehensible words, usually of a bawdy and unwholesome nature into the teeth of a gale. At the end of each line the men would shout something equally bawdy and incomprehensible back at me and would haul on the ropes.'

J. D. Doerflinger in his book, *Songs of the Sailing Days,* records one such shanty that William Small may well have sung. The shanty man's chant is in bold print, the sailors' reply in italics. The words on which the sailors pulled on the ropes are marked with an underlined stress.

I had a girl in Calio,
Pull you buggers, pull.
The hairs on her knees hung down to the floor,
For Chrissake pull.

Liverpool girls don't use no combs,
You're not pulling, you bugger.
Comb their hairs with turtle bones,
Don't tell me I'm not pulling, you prat.

I had a girl in Venezuela,
If you don't pull, I'll smash your face in
She wouldn't do it but her sister would, yea, here's the Captain!
Pull! You buggers, pull.

William, though he was later to draw on his experiences at sea for his great maritime symphonies, found the cruelty and hardships an anathema.

'The weevils were full of biscuits, the ship's cook was a scurvy old man who washed his bandages in our soup, and the mate used to lock the most handsome of the sailors in his cabin and force him to play "Mornington Crescent" with him whilst listening to the ship's black joiner singing "Bad Penny Blues". It was more than flesh and blood could stand.

'We took on a consignment of concertinas at the Turks and Cacos Islands, and in the teeth of a terrible gale stowed them and the nancy boys below. The nancy boys got at the concertinas and started playing them when we were forty leagues from land. There was a hideous row, not fitted for a Christian soul to bear. The wailing of the concertinas drowned out even the lashing of the waves and the howling of the wind.

'"We'll all have rough passages tonight," bawled the bo'sun.

'"Speak for yourself, dearie," came a voice through the grating.

'The waves were sixty foot high, I lashed myself to the mast. The mate lashed himself to the cook and in the eye of that storm I shouted every shanty I knew, and the men hauled, reefed, spliced, furled, mizzened and pumped their d...est! All to no avail. I lost my voice and in confusion the men, each convinced that his nearest companion was not pulling hard enough, started hitting each other.'

As soon as the storm abated the Captain and the men surveyed the damage. The storm had knocked off that little brass bit you have on lamps to stop the door falling open in the wind, while the men on the other hand had pulled four masts down. William Small, fearing retribution from the Captain, jumped ship in San Francisco just in time for the great earthquake.

'In San Francisco's Chinatown a violent tremor shook the streets. Trembling Chinamen filled the vermin-ridden alley-ways and malodorous thoroughfares and began hitting each other with crispy noodles and prawn crackers. I was almost blinded by the flying fragments. I smote a passing yellow man and called him a d...mnd inscrutable cur. He shouted "borox" at me and vanished into the general melée.'

It was in 'Frisco that William Small secured his first engagement as a professional musician, humming, whistling through his teeth and playing the spoons for Professor Likonti's famous and renowned flea circus (see plate 3).

40

'I was the sole musician and it was my job to provide the tiny mites with the musical accompaniment for Thespian, acrobatic and Terpsichorean feats. A roll on the spoons would accompany a walk along the wire, four bars of "Rocked In The Cradle Of The Deep" would provide a musical aura for a touching scene from the ballet, "The Magic Cucumber", while during the duel scene I would work myself into a frenzy of whistling, humming and spoon percussion, finishing off with three old plantation songs, "De Old Gwine Riboh", "De Riboh Gwine To Jordan" and "Where De Riboh Done Gone Gwine?"'.

William Small soon grew tired of the limitations of his job, sleeping with the cast and the jeers from the mob such as 'Not up to scratch, was it?' and 'What do you want, blood?' etc.

(Plate 3)

(Plate 4)

One night he ran away from the circus. Unfortunately, the circus ran away with him, only to escape from William in a bar in Milwaukee where, hiding inside a steam-engine driver's shirt, they caused him later that day to lose control of his steam vehicle. The ensuing commotion was recorded for posterity by a passing engraver and was printed that night in the *Milwaukee Examiner* (see plate 4).

The next ten years of William Small's life are still a mystery to researchers, though from papers and photographs it is known that he travelled through Africa where he was captured, sold into slavery and liberated again by Doctor Livingstone. He was a British spy in the Mardi's Palace, was whisked back to England where he met, courted and married Evelyn Singe-Crump in one single wet afternoon in November.

Evelyn Singe-Crump, Mrs Small the first, was an enigmatic figure. Inventor of the steam brassiere and an intrepid balloonist, she took William Small with her on a balloon trip over Billericay where they found themselves in the grip of an electric storm which resulted in the untimely death of the first Mrs Small.

'The lightning flashed and the storm raged. I tried to calm our spirits by playing "The Flight of the Bumble Bee" on the Jew's harp. I played on desperately for hours, through that terrible storm until my lips grew black and swollen and my tongue began to bleed. Unable to continue playing, I tried to keep my wife's mind off the desperate state of affairs by juggling with words. I showed her fourteen rhymes for Japanese lacquer, but to no avail for she grew despondent and distressed. I tried to restrain her, but in her desperation she proved too strong for me and climbed out onto the skin of the balloon where, as she clung to the netting, a bolt of lightning struck her causing

41

(Plate 5)

her steam brassiere to explode, killing her instantly. I took four grains of laudanum and collapsed in a swoon. When I came to, I was being dragged across a field by my braces which were entangled in the horns of a cow' (see plate 5).

42

It wasn't long before William Small was on the road again, appearing in Adolph's Whistling Follies on the pier at Llandudno where he met and married Miss Vesta Sparkbrook. The second Mrs Small was a petite, demure, moustachioed strong-lady who could stop shunting engines with her head and troops of mounted foot with her enormous bosoms.

The second Mrs Small proved, however, to be a harridan, refusing to let William play with his collection of stick-insects in bed, and insisting that he eat his dinner at the table, and not on the floor as was his want.

It was not long before the Smalls hit upon hard times. Adolph's Whistling Follies were disbanded overnight, when Adolph ran off with the troupe's money, disguised as Oliver Hardy with a maidservant from the Hotel Excelsior, Sunderland. Underneath her giant golfing umbrella, they made their way from the Sunderland Coco and Temperance Rooms, where the band had been appearing, to the coast where a small fishing-lugger took them to the Hook of Holland. The newspaper headlines the next morning read: 'GOLLY, FOLLIES LOLLY GOES OFF UNDER A BROLLY WITH OLLY AND POLLY'.

Small's diary for the time records:

'We were so reduced in our circumstances that when we'd used the last of our winter coals, we sandpapered each other in order to keep warm.'

William Small took to the streets, playing a gypsy violin on the cobbles of Manchester and Liverpool. In the terrible winter of that year he composed his first symphonies, 'The Maritime Symphony' and 'The Erotica Symphony' and two concertos, 'The Concerto For A Flugelhorn and Crabshells' and, perhaps the most famous of all, 'The Concerto For Woodwind And Tram'. The following year Small took ship again, this time with his first Small Orchestra, aboard the Titanic on its maiden voyage.

'We were overjoyed at securing the appointment. Little did we know that our first audience was to be a polar-bear. We billed ourselves as The William Small Small Orchestra and Gypsy Band. When our turn to play came, we made our way to the first-class saloon and had begun playing selections from Hoffman and Sousa when a grinding noise rent the ship.

'The cry "Iceberg!" sounded throughout the vessel. A distraught steward ran forward and perceiving us to be dressed in gypsy costume, and assuming that we were in fact Romanies, began making rowing movements while pointing to the floor.

"Is it a film or is it a book?" asked the first flugelhorn player.

"Three Men in a Boat?" guessed the mandolin player, who usually won at charades.

"Pillocks!" shouted the steward.

"Never heard of it," mumbled the percussionist, "it must be one of those modern books where a game-keeper interferes with the lady of the house."

"Nonsense," said the viola player, "it's that new play by that bearded vegetarian, the chap who's invented that new language, Desperanto. It's that play about the Salvation Army woman that gets burnt at the stake."

'They were still arguing as the bandstand floated out of the saloon with us aboard it, into the darkness and tragedy of that night.'

Eventually landing on an iceberg, William Small's Small Orchestra carried on playing in order to fulfill their contractual obligations.

'It was the only way we could make sure of getting paid. For fourteen days we floated on that island of ice through the violent and lurid skies of the northern icy

43

(Plate 6)

wastes, playing every tune in our repertoire many times over to an audience of penguins and polar-bears. Eventually our iceberg struck land on the rocky coast of Alaska, where we staggered ashore, demented and weary.'

In Alaska the orchestra received a less than rapturous welcome. The gold-miners of the Yukon had been expecting a consignment of chorus girls, when they found instead that the ship was not a ship but a bandstand, and that the bandstand contained not fourteen voluptuous and willing women, but six emaciated, starving, and slightly unhinged gypsies. They beat them round the town with pick-axe handles and prospecting pans.

In the Yukon, William Small disbanded his first Small Orchestra and to keep himself from starvation, took a job playing piano in the Hanging Taxman Saloon in Skagway, a drinking den which the prospectors coming in from the icy deserts would make for like a beacon in order to slake their thirsts at the end of the day. It was frequented by some of the toughest men in the Yukon. Small's diary records:

'There was one unfortunate called No Hope Jake, who for drinks would tear the nails out of the very floor-boards with his teeth and juggle with burning penguins. Another madman called Nervous McGrew had lost his wits by chewing the lead paint off his toy soldiers. McGrew would bite any woman he saw on the buttocks, shouting "All that meat and no gravy". Yet these two were harmless in their way, unlike Unpredictable Eric who would shoot any man whose name began with a vowel or a diphthong.'

No Hope Jake and Nervous McGrew were killed one night whilst returning from a New Year party, when they fell out over who was to steer the rail bogeytrain that was bringing them home (see plate 6). An event that was celebrated in a famous poem by the poet of the Yukon, Robert Service:

THE DEATH OF NO HOPE JAKE
AND NERVOUS McGREW

They tell the tales of the deserts,
And the sailors who sail on the blue,
But none could compare to that wild mad pair,
No Hope Jake and Nervous McGrew.

In the frozen northern outback,
Where men go mad for gold,
McGrew and Jake came home one night late
From a party, so it has been told.

When a man's soul shrinks to the size of a pea,
And the stars burn like holes in a blanket,
Nervous McGrew and No Hope Jake,
Got on a bogey and started to crank it.

They were full of fire water that night,
As the moon rose over the ice pole,
'I want to steer' said Nervous McGrew,
No Hope Jake kicked him right in the parcel.

A fight, a blow, a sneer, a curse,
Both men were to-the-death fighters,
Nervous McGrew bit Jake on the thigh,
And set fire to his tights with his lighter.

A bang! And a crack! As the bogey rolled on,
Nearing the edge of the precipice,
A thousand foot drop! Unable to stop!
The bogey shot over the edifice.

They lay minus legs, arms fractured, skulls broke,
And just before everything turned black,
'All right, you win' said Nervous McGrew,
'You steer going and I'll steer it back.'

It was in the Yukon that fate struck William Small a cruel blow when, during a melée at the Hanging Taxman Saloon, someone shouted: 'Shoot the piano!'

Hairy Kneed McGurk emptied his revolver into the instrument, which exploded in a shower of woodworm and dust.

'I fell to the floor in a swoon and when I came to I was curious to find that I could only talk in rhyme. An affliction which has remained with me ever since.'

A week later in an explosion in the Chinese laundry where Small worked as a shirt-flap lifter, he lost both legs and all ten fingers.

'I was at my lowest ebb. The owner of the saloon told me he would keep my job open, but I feared the worst.'

Small was lucky enough to meet a German professor of medical science who had come to the Yukon to try his luck in the gold-fields. Every claim he had made had proved to yield nothing but fool's gold. His failure drove him to drink, and in order to pay for his habit he had to help out as an engineer to the mining contractors. He made Small a prosthesis which fitted over each of his hands.

'It enabled me, after a little practice, to play perfectly and almost immediately I composed what I regard as my greatest symphony - "The Tin Fingers Saxaphone Symphony"' (see plate 7).

The fingers were worked by steam and Small's playing became a celebrated curiosity of the day. Word spread and William Small became an international figure, leaving the Yukon to travel the United States, Canada and Europe, giving lantern slide talks and moving model nude demonstrations of his travels. He appeared before all the crowned heads of Europe. His diary recalls:

(Plate 7)

'I appeared before all the crowned heads of Europe.'

He became a friend to the Great. George Bernard Shaw, Virginia Woolf, the Sackville-Wests, H. G. Wells, William Morris, Rosetti and Edmund Fink. Small was companion and friend to each and every one of them. It was at this period that he formed the last, and most famous, of his orchestras, The William Small Small Orchestra Society and Strolling Players. The line-up was Eddie Krantz - flugalhorn; Skeets Bawldry - percussion; Joe Mangionni - double bass; Sonny Bolo - vibes; Toots Matel - saxophone; Earl Jones - trombone; Kid White - banjo; and William Small - keyboard, doubling saxophone and vocals (see plate 8). Over the next twenty years they made more than forty recordings and appeared throughout the empire. His diary recalls:

'In Hawaii the entire band contacted Krantz disease. They took hold of Krantz and beat him senseless with his flugalhorn case.'

In spite of his success, a melancholy took possession of William Small. With his steam-powered fingers, he was regarded as an oddity rather than as a serious musician.

'The end,' he wrote cryptically in his diary that year, 'is not far away.'

It must have been a premonition for only a month later, while playing before the dissecting team of the Royal College of Surgeons in the Albert Hall, Ecclefechan, disaster struck (see plate 9). Kid White recorded in his autobiography, *You Lucky Plucker:*

(Plate 9)

(Plate 8)

'We were going through the slow movements of "The Legless Concerto". Everything so far had been going real well. The audience had gone wild over "Tin Fingers Symphony" and had been boogying in the aisles during "How High The Moon" and "The Maritime Concerto".

'I was extemporizing a pattern in nine-eight time, overlaying some twelve-thirteen patterns that Skeets was laying down. We knew something was wrong when the governor hollered out, "More coal, more coal!"

'We usually played that piece laid well back. The governor was laying it down like it had never been laid before. Wopping, bopping, the joint was hopping! We was blowing fit to bust a gut. The governor was standing on his stool, sweating and yelling and moving and grooving. Steam was coming out of the joints in his fingers. He gave a shout, the band gave him a break, he played so fast the piano caught fire. There was a bang, the lights went out and when they came back on again there was nothing, just steam everywhere and one eyelash, and the kid who shovelled the coal into the boiler had no hair left.'

The eyelash was buried in the Small's family plot in Staffordshire. The route from the church to the cemetery was lined by more than three hundred and fifty people as William Small and his Small Orchestras became, on that day a thing of memory only. The empire and the world of music bade farewell to the man who was possibly one of the greatest composers England has ever known - William Small.

47

Repossessing the video, 1876.

I'M IN LOVE WITH THE CHECK-OUT GIRL AT TESCO'S

'Twas a cold November day
When I made my way
To the supermarket down on the high street.
I got me some corned beef,
Corn-on-the-cob so sweet and
Some corn plasters for muh gran'ma's feet.
And it was then I met the lady
Who damn near drove me crazy.
When I saw her my body felt a thrill,
My heart went pitter patter
And my teeth began to chatter
When I saw that sweet thing ringin' up the till.

Chorus
I'm in love with the check-out girl at Tesco's,
She's the sweetest thing I've ever seen,
And every afternoon I'm standing in the queue,
Hoping she'll handle my baked beans.

I stood there by the freezer,
And I swear I tried to please her,
I smiled at her and tried to talk real nice;
But she hardly gave a mutter
As she checked my cheese and butter
And looked at me with eyes as cold as ice.
Well, my heart was nearly breaking
So I went back for some bacon,
Some skinless sausage and a box of crackers,
And I stood there like a fool in that supermarket queue
With melted ice-cream running down my legs.

I even bought fish fingers
Just so's I could linger
And watch her fingers working on the keys.
I was burning hot with passion
As she fingered through my rations,
I could feel the butter running down my knees.
I went back six times or more,
Bought Oxo's by the score,
Margarine, and a pair of bedroom slippers.
I asked for her phone number
As she wrapped up my cucumber,
And she hit me with a packet of frozen kippers.

Well, I see her in my dreams,
Stood by the clotted cream.
And we kiss and hug down alleyways of cornflakes,
And we cuddle and we kiss
By the smokey bacon crisps,
And I wake up broken-hearted when the dawn breaks.
And I'm spending all my money
On custard, soap and honey,
But I know that sweet thing will never be mine.
And as she wraps another jar of pickles
The tears begin to trickle -
'Cos she's twenty-one, and me I'm only nine!

The Rudeparts of Omar Khayyam

THE THREE-LEGGED PIG

As I was goin' on a walk one day
I saw a pig in a sty,
I looked in as the pig lay there
And I swear that it's no lie:
The pig had only three legs
And where the fourth should be
Was a hand-carved peg-leg made from brass
And tipped with ivory!

Well, the farmer he came passin' by,
I said: 'Farmer, tell to me,
How come that pig 'stead of having four
Legs has only three?'
Well, he scratched his head with a pitch-fork
And sat down on a log,
Sayin': 'Son, I got to tell you
That's no ordinary hog!

'Two years last fall the old school bus,
On the hill it lost its brakes,
Chockful of kids, shot down the hill
And the bus went into the lake.
Well, the kids were cryin', thought they were dyin',
Well, that pig in the lake it dived,
Dragged every kid out and with his snout
Gave them the kiss of life.

'Just last spring I was huntin' coon,
It rained all day and night.
Got home soaked, took off muh clothes,
Laid 'em on the stove to dry.
In the middle of the night the clothes took alight,
Smoke knocked out me and the wife,
Through smoke and flames that old hog came,
That old hog saved our lives.

'Just last berry time muh grandson,
A child just one year old,
Was a-playin' in the hogweed,
Wandered on the railroad.
Old 49 came down the line,
All we could do was pray,
We were cryin' when the pig went flyin'
And dragged that child away.'

'Well, farmer,' I said, 'I thank you
For the story of the wonderful pig!
And wherever I go, I'll let everyone know
Of the wonderful things he did,
But that still don't explain the peg-leg.'
The farmer said: 'You dunce,
That wonderful pig - after all it did -
We couldn't eat it all at once!'

"Honest, I'll only put it in a bit"

A Short Guide to Modern Architecture

Modern architecture was invented by Le Corbusier, a Frenchman who rejected completely such old-fashioned ideas as curves, niches, balustrades, crenellations and flying buttresses.
He discovered that if you can make one man miserable by putting him in a box like this:

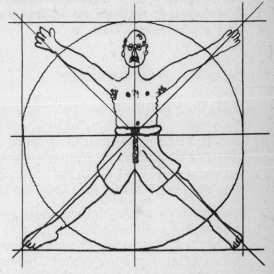

then you can make a lot more people miserable by putting them in a lot more boxes like these:

The end result, as we all know, is Milton Keynes, Easterhouse, Sheffield's Hyde Park housing estate, and the centre of every major European city that architects and planners have managed to get their blighting little mitts on, including the Paris Pompidou Centre, the only building I know with all the plumbing on show.

Two years ago I appeared, dressed as a priest, on Granada Television to deliver an address on the subject of town planners and architects. This is it:

Dear Beloved Brethren

Tonight's reading is from Barbarians 1984.

And it came to pass that there were in those days certain men who had their brains taken out and were named the planners. And they did go forth and meet the high priests of stupidity in their council chambers and they did take the city and they did cock it up.

They did go into the highways and byways with their measures and their chains. They did take the length and breadth thereof and they looked at the city and they did say, 'Let us knock it down. Let us move the people to the wasteland and the deserts, for forty years let them wander, let them be visited with plagues. Let the first plague be water running down the walls.

'Let the second plague be badly fitting doors and windows, let them be cold and damp. Let the third plague be a plague of social workers.

'Let the people have sore sicknesses. Let their children peer from windows. Let the winds howl about their dwellings and let them be infested with rats and vermin.

'Let the people have no work. And let them also have no hope.'

And it came to pass as the planners said for they were strong and the people were weak.

And the God of the planners was Corbusier and they did worship him. In his image and likeness did they build. Many cubits high were their towers and great was the fear of all who dwelt in them. For he did say to the builders and the scribes, 'Take ye a man and measure him. Now take the lines thereof and make a box.' And it was done and it was called a module and then the Lord Corbusier said, 'Build many modules and into them put many men.' And it was done as the Lord said.

And although the planners did build thereof they dwelt not in their towers. For they did dwell in faraway lands where there were village halls, thatched roofs, private schools, BMW cars, and preservation societies. In

54

green pastures they did lie and of milk, honey, Muscadet and paté from Sainsbury's they did eat.

And the planners did say, 'Thou shalt build a temple to Mammon the God of Greed. No windows shall it have, of straight lines shall it be builded. And the rents to the merchants within shall be so high people shall pay more for their goods. Of pots and tiles shall thou cover it, yea, so that it looketh like a mighty urinal, and it shall be called 'The New Town Centre'. Thou shalt put up a craven image by a modern sculptor that no one shall understand and which shall be covered with aerosol and blasphemies.

And, yea, thou shalt have necks of solid brass so that thou shalt ignore the people's shouts when they cry 'My God what pillock hath designeth this - my kid brother could do better than that with his Lego.' And lo, it came to pass as they said and their necks were of solid brass and they did build it. And the people did cry, 'Lord, we need houses and homes.' And lo, the planners did build offices. And they did stand empty.

'Lord,' cried the people, 'we need homes.' And lo, the planners did build more offices. And they did stand empty.

And a third time the people cried out and a third time the planners did ignore them and did build offices and they did stand empty.

And lo, the people wept but they were not heard for they were as voices crying in the wilderness. And the architects had many shekels and did laugh all the way to the counting house.

And lo, the cities were as dead places and the wind did howl through them and at night they were empty and without hope.

The planner is my shepherd. He maketh me to walk; through dark tunnels and underpasses he forceth me to go. He maketh concrete canyons tower above me. By the rivers of traffic he maketh me walk. He knocketh down all that is good, he maketh straight the curves. He maketh of the city a wasteland and a car park.

He giveth over the city to the motor car. He annointeth my head with their stink and their noise assaulteth my ears. Yea, the planner is my shepherd, he maketh me to live in concrete hovels, in the abomination of desolation he maketh me to go. He maketh me to lie down in concrete pastures.

Yea, though I walk through the valley of the shadow of mismanagement and the depths of stupidity, I shall fear no evil save more of the same. By the ribbon development where I lay down, how I shall weep when I remember Ancoats, Hulme, Darn Hill, Hattersley, Netherley, Huyton, Skelmersdale, Easterhouse, Hyde Park, Peterlee, Milton Keynes, etc. etc.

As a point of interest, after the broadcast not one single planner or architect wrote in to defend their actions. The only letters came from people who were furious about me doing it dressed as a priest.

FALL-OUT CALYPSO

De odder day I got a big shock,
A ting come in troo me letterbox,
A Gobberment paper wid lots ob tips,
'Bout what to do in de Apocalypse.

Chorus
Fall-out calypso, fall-out calypso,
Tings fallin' out all over de place,
De hair an' de teef, de nose an' de knees,
But de Gobberment tell us we'll be okay.

But when it come to de radiation,
Spreadin' about all troo de nation,
I grab me tackle an' run helter-skelter,
Lookin' for de Gobberment fall-out shelter.

I say to de man I want to hide,
He say but dere's no room inside.
It full up wit MPs an' Lord Mayors,
You better go home, hide under de stairs.

Down in town dere's a hole in de ground,
Where a million cibil serbants can be found.
Dey'll be dere on Apocalypse Day
Fillin' in de forms in triplicate.

De paper say when de sirens roar
Climb in de cupboard an' close de door,
Put de head between de knees and close de eye,
Den you can kiss your ass-'ole goodbye.

When de dust has settled all around
And de Gobberment crawl out from a hole in de ground,
If you got locked out ob de fall-out shelter,
If you can do de jigsaw puzzles you can put yourself togedder.

*Cholmondley was the first
white man ever to set eyes on a
Weetabix fountain.*

Effects of farting in a diving suit, parts 1 to 3.

Soup Collecting for Fun and Profit

Never forget that you can do things with a slice of lemon, a spoonful of olive oil, and a courgette that will leave the family helpless with laughter, but could get you arrested. A radish, lightly grated into a glass of Guinness, provides an interesting aperitif, particularly before a dish of Mexican food - but don't stand near any naked flames for at least forty-eight hours afterwards.

HOW TO EAT WELL ON FOUR POUNDS A WEEK

Living in straitened circumstances does not mean that you must have a bland or uninteresting diet. Think of the dishes you could prepare from the materials, vegetables and plants that are all around you in everyday life:

Privet Mousse
Tadpole Meunière
Rat au Poivre
Wellington Wellington
Risotto de UB40
Escalopes de Ginger Tom en Papillotes
Croquettes de Chickweed
Oeufs Sparrow Fines Herbes
Champignons Mur Humide

And probably the pièce de la resistance:

Hearing Aids in Chocolate.

THIS WEEK'S RECIPE: ANDALUSIAN TOE-NAIL SOUP

2 gross Andalusian Toe-nails
1 cup of warm water
1 pinch of nutmeg
1 pinch of flour
1 pinch of coriander
1 lump of butter
2 onions
1 packet of Rennies

Fry the onions and lightly sear the toe-nails in the butter making sure they don't stick. Add the rest of the stuff, light blue touch-paper - and retire eating Rennies and shouting 'Olé!'

SOME THINGS THE GROWN-UPS JUST WON'T TELL YOU

Why doesn't a ball stay up there
When you throw it up in the air?
That tortoise that we've got at school
Why doesn't it grow hair?
I wish I knew the answers,
I don't think that it's fair.
There's some things that the grown-ups just won't tell you.

Why don't little ball-bearings
Grow up to be big?
Why can't you get bits of bacon
And make them back into pig?
They say they don't know the answers,
But I think that that's a fib.
There's some things that the grown-ups just won't tell you.

Where does all the fluff come from
You find between your toes?
How do those big bogeys
Climb inside your nose?
They must come in the night
When you're asleep, I suppose.
There's some things that the grown-ups just won't tell you.

Does God go to the toilet?
And what gives you a cough?
Why don't fish get rusty?
What puts the smell in your socks?
If you undid your belly-button,
Would your bum really fall off?
There's some things that the grown-ups just won't tell you.

Why doesn't rain fall sideways?
Or even upside down?
Where do the stars go in the daytime?
Why do worms live underground?
You eat food all different colours,
Why does it all come out brown?
There's some things that the grown-ups just won't tell you.

Billericay Ladies massed maraca team were the highlight of the Pope's visit.

Some Modern Types

I'm a punk poet, right? Know wha' I mean? Went to the local grammar school like, but I don't want nobody to know tha' I went there really because it'd destroy me street credibility. Me mam sent me to elocution lessons from when I was seven to when I was eleven, but I decided I'd never get on in the punk world if I talked posh, so what I did is I went walking round the back streets, round Woolworth's, Tesco, C & A and really rough places like that until I was able to pick up the accents of all the proles hobbling round with their shopping bags. Anyway, it's great to be here on this anti-racist, gay whales against the bomb concert, and what I'm going to do for you now is do a poem wha' I wrote which is appearing on me latest biscuit tin and it's called '**I MET A TART IN THE FAT MAN'S DISCO'.**

Sipping cups of coffee
In a dive just off the park,
Transylvanian terrors
Are truckin' through the dark,
And in the crapulous alleys
Where the cats are scared to go,
Even the Constable Plods
Say the area's a no no.
From the juke in the greasy cafe
Comes a slick, sick sleazy jangle
Soundin' like a tom-cat
With its balls caught in a mangle.
Down the town the taxis spew them
Out into the disco,
Fat men looking for totties
Ready to go 'a-go-go'.
The salesmen from the big hotel,
Their bellies balloons of flesh
Are rotund little Romeos
Toupeed Valentinos fresh
From their sample-filled Cortinas
With the jackets in the back,
Ninety-five in the outside lane -
'Bugger you, Jack!'
They wobble on to the dance floor,
Full of gin and tonic,
What do they look like?
Bloody chronic!
They phoned home, 'I'm working late,
I won't be driving back.'
The only thing he's working on is his patter,
And that's crap!
He's cruising now, sweating like a pig,
His heart thumps like a tom tom,
He cops, she smiles, he gives thumbs up
To his mate who says, 'Yer on, John.'
He takes her back, gives her a drink,
Gives her a line and then
Gives her room service, gives her a fag,
Gives her a drink again,
Gives her a second helping,
And then as cool as you please
Gives her her taxi fare back home -
In return she gives him ...herpes.

Fankyew.

John Clarke

DED END KIDZ TUES

Fri THE PRITZ WANKER ZZ TOPS

Fr O' Driscol ...

Now, boys, I want you to put away your books, put your hands on the top of your desks, sit up straight and listen carefully because I am going to say something very important to you. Chewing, Johnson - in the bin. Now, boys, when you've been getting ready for games or when you've been in the changing rooms getting ready for rugger, or when you've been getting ready for bed at night and getting your little jim-jams on, some of you may have noticed that there is a part of your body that makes you boys and other people not boys. Now there is nothing to be ashamed of with that little part of your body. Because God gave that part of your body to you for a purpose, and a very special purpose it is indeed.

And what I want to talk about now is your little bodies and the special part that special part may play in your lives. There is nothing to be ashamed of with your bodies at all. 'Cause didn't God be after giving them to us so we'd have something to keep our immortal souls in? Now your bodies, boys. I want you to think of your bodies as though your bodies were just like a bus, just like those big red buses that you get on your way home from school. Now if the bus is your body, then the engine is your little heart, pumping away to give you the energy to go down the road, and your legs are like the bus wheels taking you along. So there's your heart pumping away to give you the energy and there's your legs taking ya back home at night after you've had a hard day at school playing rugger on the field and doing French conjugations, Latin quotations and Pythagoras' theorem. So there it is, you've got your body the bus, and your heart the little engine, and your legs the wheels. Now as you know every bus has a driver, now the driver of your bus is of course your soul. Now God has given you your soul, he's put it inside your body. Nobody can see where your soul is, just as on the bus you don't know whether things are upstairs or downstairs necessarily, though of course at any one time some of them must be. Now your soul is there inside your body like an invisible driver on the bus and it's taking you down the road of Life, only in this case not back from home but to Heaven we hope, although as you all know there are other places the bus stops at, Limbo, Purgatory, and for those buses totally lost in the fog the terminal is Hell. Now the conductor of the bus is your conscience. That is to say that just as a bus has a conductor that tells the driver what's happening on the bus, how many people are on it and where he's got to go, etc. etc. So your conscience tells you - because you've been brought up good Catholic boys - exactly what to do with your little bodies. No, Gittins, the conscience does not get off and brew up at the Half-Way House. See me after for being cheeky. Now some of you boys will know that when you're coming home at night, sometimes when the bus is stopped in Piccadilly Gardens, that a lot of those drunken men from Yates's Wine Lodge carrying those bottles in the brown paper bags, sometimes will climb on the bus. And they'll cause all sorts of disruptions. They'll fall down the stairs, drop the bottles, argue with people, sing out loud, use vile curses and foul languages and they'll sometimes void the contents of their stomachs down the stairwell. Now, boys, what I want to say to you is that as you're travelling down the road of your life in your little bus with your little soul driving it and your little conductor telling you what to do, the devil will tempt you boys. Now Satan tempting you is just like the men from Yates's Wine Lodge climbing up the stairs of your bus. Now do you all understand that? Are there any questions?

And then we came home from school and me dad said 'If you want we can go' and I said 'Great, I want to go' and me brother said he wanted to go as well and me little sister Angela said she wanted to go but she was too small and me dad said she couldn't go at all, so we left her back home with me mam and we got on the bus and it cost nearly two bob for me dad to go to town and it cost us a bob each for me and our Billy and we got to town and we had a pencil and a notebook each and we went down to the station and me dad got some platform tickets and it was great because you could hear all the noise and there were people walking about and it was dead loud and dead dead dead good and we went on and we saw the 'Duke of Edinburgh' which was a namer and that was going through and me dad said that was going to Carlisle and then we saw the 'Duchess of Leinster' and that was going to North Wales me dad said and then the 'City Of Leeds' came through and that was three namers in one go and then we had a cup of tea and some biscuits in the buffet on the station and me dad had some beer and then we went back out again and we saw fourteen tank engines and it was dead dead good and we put all their numbers down in the notebooks and on the way back me dad got me and our Billy some Airfix models from a model shop in town and our Billy got an Airfix Spitfire and I got an Airfix Mustang and on the way home Billy dropped the tube of glue which he should have used to build his Airfix Spitfire from on the floor and the conductor trod on it and walked up and down the aisle with all bus tickets sticking to his feet and me dad didn't see this but I did and I said I was going to tell me dad but our Billy said I wasn't to and if I didn't tell him he'd let me have his collection of *Wizard* and *Hotspur* comics when we got back and when we got back me mam said were we hungry and we said no 'cause we were full of biscuits and tea from the railway station buffet but in any case she made us some toast and some Ovaltine and we listened to 'Journey Into Space' and I started my model but it stuck to the newspaper on the table and some glue went on the cat and it stuck to the hearth and then we went to bed and it was dead dead good. It was the best time I had ever ever.

Timothy Jones

'Spike' hughes

Take out your history books and your text books, sharpen your pencils and let's see if we can knock some of that rice pudding out of your brains that you've been stuffing in all dinner-time, those of you, that is, who weren't actually climbing over the walls of the school to get out and look at the girls from Loretto down the road going past on their way to games, and don't think I didn't see that. And by the way if any of my boys are found doing that they will find themselves defenistrate and impaled on the spikes of the school railings down below. Now can anybody tell me why Bismarck was successful in the unification of Germany in spite of the opposition of the junker classes? Are you awake, Sutcliffe, or have you found it ultimately possible to be fast asleep with your eyes fully open? I notice by the way that Harding has a new haircut. Such a haircut as I have never seen before. I believe, Harding, such a haircut is in fact called a crew cut. All I can say, Harding, is a crew cut like that reminds me of a poem I once heard:

Fuzzy Wuzzy was a bear,
Fuzzy Wuzzy had no hair,
Fuzzy Wuzzy wasn't fuzzy, wuz'ee?

Don't titter, Johnson, it doesn't become you. Particularly when your hair looks as though it's been recently used for dubbing somebody's boots. It looks as though there is a good three inches of lard clinging round the brim of your collar. Now back to Bismarck. Molloy, don't do that, boy, you'll go blind. Your father doesn't seem to be able to afford to get you a decent haircut either, so I don't see how he's possibly going to be able to afford to fork out for a pair of glasses for you. Right, come on, somebody answer the question!

69

War-time *veteran, stationed at Much Boozing In-The Marsh where he distinguished himself by flying a desk for four years. He was awarded his medal for downing a Messerschmidt 109E with a well-aimed brick. He is now running a thatched country pub near Woodstock in Oxfordshire.*

... four thousand foot, pressed the titty, duff as last year's plum-pud, baled out, ditched the kite in the drink and walked back to the 'drome. What's that, Reg? Same again? Large G and T and yours, Frank, brandy was it? Yes sir, we can do you a ploughman's. If you'd like to sit down, I'll get the young lady to bring it over to you.

No, I said to Ronald yesterday - no thanks, Jimmy, I'll stick to the old Havana if you don't mind. No, I said to Ronald, 'Well if he was a son of mine I'd damn well know what to do.' Course he didn't like it but I told him straight. I'd have got the old twelve bore out and marched the pair of them straight down the aisle. Young people today, it makes you wonder what the hell they think we're here for. They seem to think the world owes them a living! That's right, Jimmy, it's the dole, of course it is. Why should a man work for a living if he can get a good wage for nothing - a signature on a piece of paper? And there's another thing, drugs. They're trying to legalise cannabis now. I know what I'd do with the pushers - correct, Reg, hang the damn shooting match of them.

There's something wrong with people who need artificial stimulation, pumping stuff into themselves for kicks. It's bloody disgusting. Another brandy, Frank, gin and tonic for Reg and Scotch for Ron. If you need drugs then there's something the matter with you.

Time, ladies and gentlemen, please!

Wing Co Larks DFC

Admiral Bud 'Lemon Face' Krapowtski...

As Pentagon defense spokesman, can I say that we in the Pentagon understand entirely the misgivings that the people of this country have with reference to the siting of chem. psych. germ ops missiles here.

Conceptually, in a postulated ongoing war-awareness situation, Fortress Britain would be a forward logistical staging post for the introduction of chem. psych. germ ops weapons into Soviet territory. Retaliatory second-strike counter-offensive operations, directed from the President's airborne command 'centre, are a necessary part of the whole defensive base of camp Europe.

We guestimate that, retaliatorywise against the Warsaw Pact countries, we would be capable of delivering a billion mega-tons of chem. psych. germ ops missiles, the equivalent for you laymen of a million times the plague which caused the Black Death.

We believe the siting of these missiles to be imperative in the interests of Peace and that it is far better that they be over here in Europe than in the USA since you'll be zapped first. Also, we need these weapons to be produced in order that the arms manufacturers make massive profits. Also, to be perfectly honest, I'm old now and don't give a shit who gets it. Let it all go, that's what I say. Armageddon! Here I come! Particularly since I, personally, credo-wise, am a born again Christian and I believe that my place is in Heaven with the good Lord, not down here throwing smoked salmon and Blue Nun into a gang of newspaper and television defense correspondents - ya commie-lefty, bunch of peacenik scum.

Now any questions?

You can't bring that through here, it isn't allowed. No sir. I know that, but I'm given my instructions and my instructions say that you can't bring that through here. I don't care whether it's logical or not. That's got nothing to do with me, sir. I know it wouldn't hurt anybody if I let you through with it. That's not the point. Once I let one through, then that will be it. They'll all want to bring them through. Then where will we be?

Well, if you miss your train, I'm afraid that's not my affair, sir. It's more than my job's worth to let you through with that. You'll need a special form from the office. No, I don't know where you get them from. You'll have to go down to the office. I am only acting under instruction.

They may seem stupid to you, sir, and I'm sure you're entitled to your point of view, but I have to abide by the rules.

There's no need to get abusive, sir. Oh! Well, I suppose you're one of those people that doesn't think we need rules, so we can have lesbians and gays and communists running the country, are you? Well, I didn't fight in the last war to have long-haired poofs like you telling me my job.

If you want to complain to the station master, then that is your privilege, sir, and I can't stop you.

I'm sorry you're taking that attitude, sir, but there is absolutely no way you're taking that through here. No way. It's more than my job's worth. I'm only acting under instructions. You can shout and rant and rave as much as you want, sir, but it won't alter the fact one bit.

I'm locking the gate and I'm not listening to you, so there.

Eric Jobsworth

Barnyard Moaning

Barnyard Moaning is a northern comedian, not of the old cloth-cap and clogs type, however, but of the newer, brasher kind, bred in the 'scampi in the basket' belt of northern clubland. He's hard, cruel, aggressive and racist.

All his stories degrade women, humanity generally, or they attack and ridicule minority groups.

... So the Irishman says, 'How's things in Lesbania?'

You know, people accuse me of being racist. I'm not racist, in fact there's two things I can't stand, race prejudice and coons.

There's this bloke giving his wife one, when the kid comes in. He says, 'What you doing, dad?' He said, 'I'm trying to see if your mummy's got any wax in her ears.' The little boy said, 'There shouldn't be any. The milkman knocked it all out yesterday.'

My wife said to me, 'Kiss me like you did before we got married.' I says, 'All right, but don't close your legs, you'll break me glasses.'

Are you going, Missus? Find me humour offensive, do you? Do you? Well, I probably wouldn't like to see you performin' either.

No, talking about coons, I think the paddies and the coons should get together and kick shit out of the Pakistanis.

Anyway there's this nun ...

73

The Gillett family persevered
with their contact lenses.

SUBURBAN BLUES

Well, I woke up this morning,
Got me those suburban blues.
I said I woke up this morning,
Got me those suburban blues.
Electric toothbrush fell down the bidet,
Now all the lights in the house are fused.

Next door neighbour's trimmed his hedge,
Swear that I could die.
He's done it again and let his privet clippings
Fall down on my side.
The au pair's Hoovered up the hamster,
It's got stuck up the tube;
Milkman won't take Barclaycard,
What's a poor boy goin' to do?
Said Lord, got the suburban blues,
Pay your rates, pay your taxes,
Still swear to the Lord you're gonna lose!

Well, I woke up this morning,
Got me those suburban blues again.
What did I say? I said woke up this morning,
Got me those suburban blues again.
My boy dropped his Action Man down the loo,
He's blocked up all the drains!

Well, I get up every morning,
Put on my jogging togs,
Only trouble is Suburbia
Got lots and lots of dogs.
Jogging down the pavement,
Slippin' and sliding through the rain,
I hear the neighbours say:
'There he goes! Drunk again!'
Oh Lord, got the suburban blues,
Pay your rates, pay your taxes,
Still swear to the Lord you're gonna lose!

Said good morning, blues,
Blues, how do you do?
Said good morning, blues,
Blues, how do you do?
Skinheads put the garden gnomes
In the plastic Alpine pool.

Gypsy woman told my momma
'Fore I was born:
'Boy child's gonna be lucky
If you buy this rabbit-foot charm.'
I wore my lucky rabbit's foot, thought
Life was a bed of roses.
Now I'm the only man in Suburbiton
With myxomatosis!
Oh Lord, got the suburban blues,
Pay your rates, pay your taxes,
Still swear to the Lord you're gonna lose.

Exploitation of children, No. 6. A flying post child (of The Aerodrome Babies).

JUST CAN'T BEAT THIS FAMILY LIFE

Granny's in the bathroom smokin' dope,
Been there four hours, says she's lookin' for the soap.
Smoke's comin' out through the bathroom door,
The cats lyin' stoned on the landing floor.

Chorus
Don't you give me no trouble,
Don't give me no strife,
'Cos you just can't beat this family life.

Sister's window has a big red light,
Lots of men friends every night;
Ladder runs up to her window-sill,
All you can hear is the ringin' of her till.

Up in the attic is little brother Tom,
Trying to make a neutron bomb,
Been playing with his chemistry set for years,
That's why little sister's got four ears.

Mother put an axe in the rentman's head,
Buried in the cellar, no-one knows he's dead;
Gonna call her Mother Hubbard,
So many bones in the family cupboard.

Daddy goes out 'most every night,
Climbing roofs in the pale moonlight;
They say he's like Robin Hood a bit,
'Cos he robs from the rich and keeps it.

Grandad's made his own moonshine
From metal polish and turpentine;
The dog drank some and started to cough,
Sparks from its ass and its fur fell off.

He can't hear you, he's got his willy in his ear.

K-TEL FOLK SONG

Come all ye rambling account-i-ants
And listen to my story,
It's only a thousand verses long
I hope it doesn't bore ye.
As I roved out in Wool-i-worth's
To get some elastic bands,
As I was passing the pick 'n' mix
I was jumped on by a press-gang.

For forty days our ship was tossed
All in the Bay of Biscay;
The captain was tossed, all the men was tossed,
I was sick myself in an ashtray.
We landed at Crimeas shore
And in no time at all,
I lost an arm, a leg and an eye and me Sony personal stereo
With the help of a cannon-ball.

I went back to old Eng-i-land
And was constrained to beg,
Cos there's not much call for a Bow Street Runner
Who only has one leg.
Me and four more, out poaching went
Into Lord Scrotum's park,
And caught we was by gamekeepers -
We should have gone in the dark!

Transported we was to Botany Bay
On far Australia's shore,
But I disguised myself as a kangaroo
And jumped ship at Krakatoa.
I was lying down and having a kip,
The sun was shining grand,
Then a big volcano went 'boom! bang! crack!'
It went off in me hand.

It blew me up into the air
And far across the briny,
I got up so high I could see the sun,
It was big and shiny.
Then my progress, it reversed itself
Because the air was steep,
And I fell back down as far as I'd come
And landed in the deep.

I was about to drown from breathing water,
When to my surprise,
I was escorted to the surf-i-ess
By a pretty mer-i-maid.
I was picked up by a whaling fleet
And in search of whales did go,
I told them it was next to Eng-i-land
But they did not want to know.

These whales was very enormous fish,
The captain was most courageous,
He said he'd once caught Moby Dick,
I said I hoped it wasn't contagious.
Then I found meself adrift at sea
When the ship went down in a gale,
And I was just about to start eatin' meself
When I was eaten meself by a whale.

For forty days I roamed the earth
In that Leviathan's old belly,
I must admit I've had better lodgings,
And some that weren't so smelly.
I determined to escape by rolling up in a ball
And giving him constipation,
There was a bang and a crack, I shot out of the back
In the middle of Blackpool illuminations.

And there I met my own true love
As I was walking on the sands.
She was hiding in a little tent
With a Punch and Judy in her hands.
I crept up in behind the tent,
So quiet she would not know it,
And I put a smile on her crocodile
Saying 'That's the way to do it!'

So come all you rambling wheelbarrow designers,
And warning take by me,
Don't spend your money on women and booze
When you haven't got any!
And here's a good piece of advice
I got from an optimist:
Always remember a bird in the hand
Does it on your wrist!

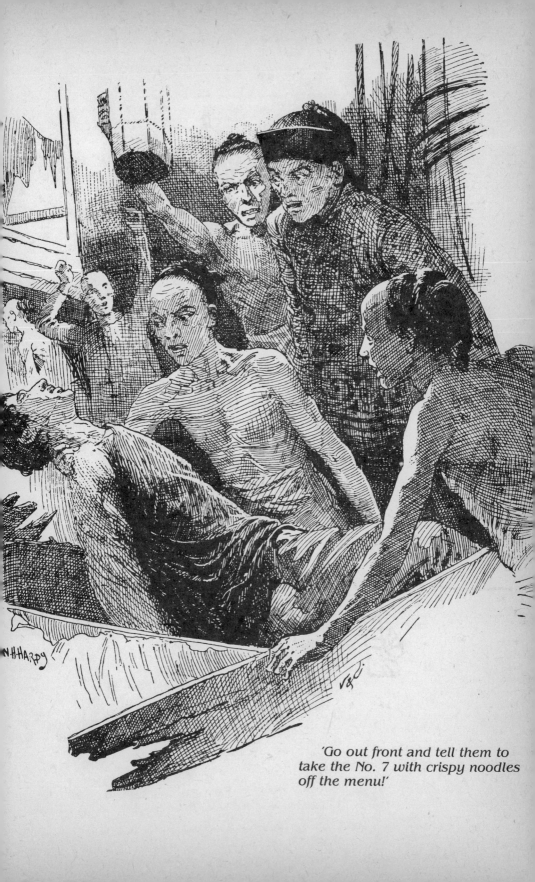

'Go out front and tell them to take the No. 7 with crispy noodles off the menu!'

The Leaning Pee of Towser

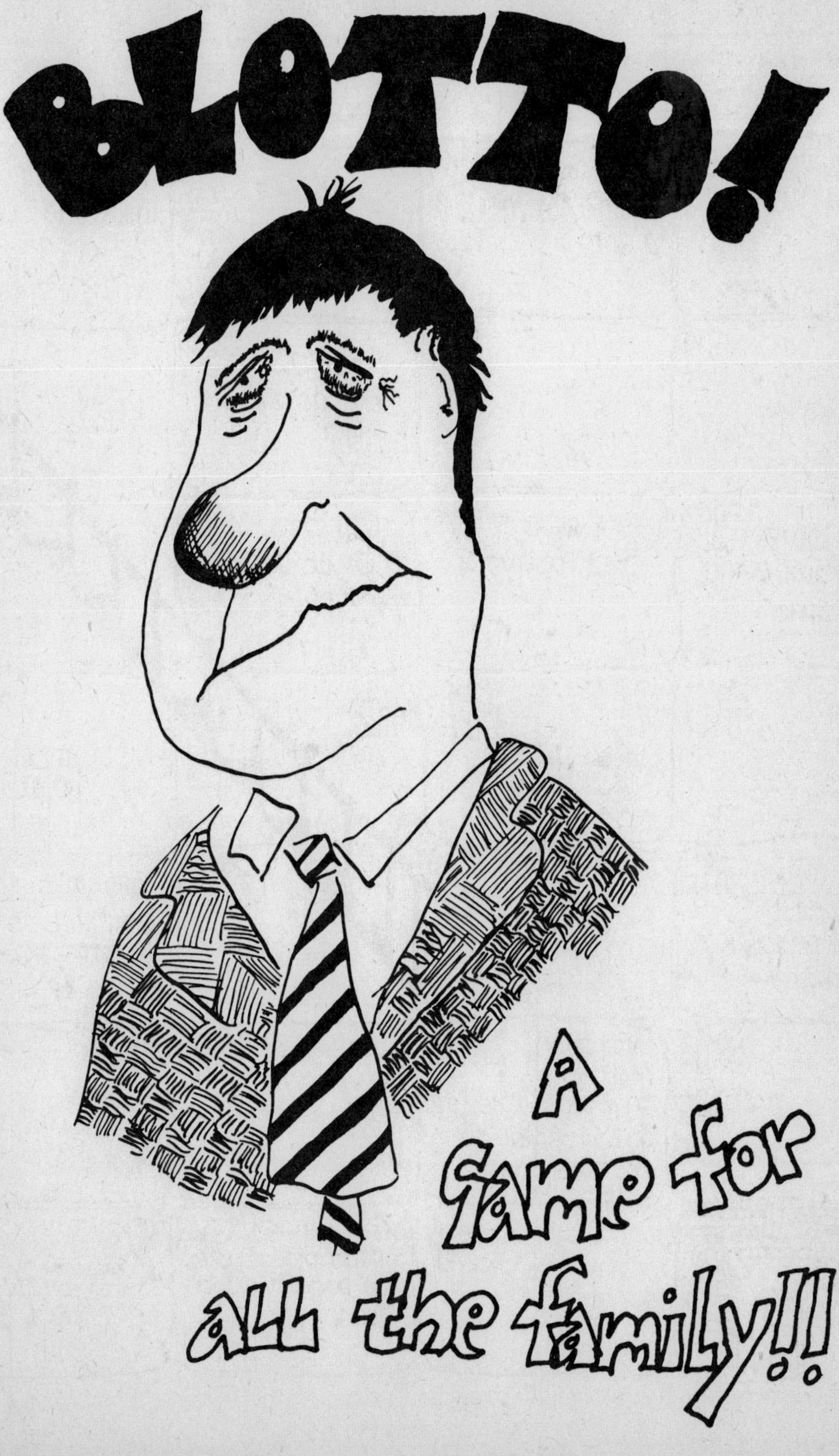
BLOTTO!
A
Game for
ALL the family!!

BLOTTO RULES OK?

1 You will need a pair of dice, some beer bottle-tops and matches or crisps to use as counters.
2 No more than fifty and no less than one player may take part.
3 Gouging, biting and ear-twisting are not permissible moves.
4 Each player has to throw a seven to start.
5 Any number thrown over eight counts as three, unless it's nine or eleven, in which case it counts as the number first thrown minus seven.
6 Players who land at the top of a set of stairs 'fall down' them shouting 'Blotto!' Players who land on a lift square shout 'What floor is it?' and follow the lift back to the lift square directly above.
7 If more than one player lands on the same square, then both or all players must sing one verse of one of the following songs:
Delilah
Show Me The Way To Go Home
You'll Never Walk Alone
If I Ruled The World
Danny Boy
8 The winner, who shall be deemed that person who first lands on square one hundred, shall buy all the other players a drink for being such a smart-arse.

The Riddle of the Sphincter

The Archbishop and his dog Jim.

HOW TO MAKE YOUR FORTUNE FROM WRITING BOOKS

Writing books is a very good way of making a crust or two since, once the initial work has been done and notes scribbled hastily on the back of bus tickets have become fully fledged tomes, you simply sit back and wait for the royalties to trickle in. It may be only at the rate of a few pence a year, but the consoling thought at the back of your mind must be that it's trickling in without you ever having to get your tochas off the tuffet.

If you want to make a fortune from writing books steer clear of short stories, books on esoteric subjects such as *Inkwells Of The World* and, in particular, eschew like the Black Death books of poetry. You may well be a sensitive soul who thrills to the murmuring of brooks and the first glimpse of eyebright in an early spring meadow, but frankly the rest of the world doesn't give a bugger. If you write a slim volume of verse with a title culled from the line of a Shakespeare play such as *Out Brief Candle, Where The Bee Sucks,* or *For This Relief Horatio,* then there is not a bookie in the land that will give you odds against it still gathering dust on the top shelves in the stockrooms of Smith's and Menzies five years later.

Books that will make you money, however, are sex and violence novels, text books, books on gardening, the royal family, dogs, cooking, and war. If you could write a book that combines all these elements you would probably never have to pick up a Parker for the rest of your chuff.

'Oh Fudge!' said Her Majesty, kicking one of the corgis across the limestone pavement at Malham Cove. In the distance the sound of mortar shells crackled ominously over the sandstone outcrops and the carboniferous limestone with its clinks and grykes and rare spring saxifrage.

A major from the catering corps, half his face a mass of scar tissue and congealed blood, had cracked six eggs into a bowl and was whisking them strongly before pouring the mixture over a previously cooked Armenian vegetarian dish of two onions chopped and lightly fried with a clove of garlic in some olive oil, into which had been dropped four sliced courgettes, three tomatoes, a sprinkling of chopped mushrooms, some grated goat's cheese and a pinch of fresh coriander and chilli powder.

'Good afternoon, Your Majesty,' he muttered standing to attention. She smiled at him then a movement in the valley below caught her eye. A lusty peasant fellow lay athwart the thighs of a milkmaid. Her camisole lay on the grass beside him and his hot lips moved passionately across her, etc. etc. etc.

Humorous books can sell well if they are promoted properly. This usually involves the author going to London, getting up at 5 am and entering a studio full of insomniacs, where he sits under hot lights for three hours, listens to the news and weather sixteen times over, gets dragged into a discussion on the advantages or disadvantages of pre-packaging dried milk, and talks about his book for two minutes.

When promoting books publishers also like to take the author and drive him round all the local radio stations where he will appear on programmes with disc jockeys, many of whom have:

a)Never heard of him
b)Haven't read the book
c)Don't give a bugger.

'Well, that was 'Kiss Kiss' from Wham Bam and the Thank You Mams. It's two o'clock on Wednesday 13 August on wonderful downtown Radio Gibberdilly and right here in the studio is Elphinstone Drinkpootle to talk about his latest book The Consumer's Guide to Death. Now, Elphinstone, do you really think it's possible to be funny about death?'

'It's a serious book about the price of coffins.'

'Oh, fine ... well, we'll be back to talk to Elphinstone again right after this.'

A good way of writing a humorous book without doing much in the way of writing at all - it will only take you a few minutes a day - is exemplified in The Arthur Boot Letters. Arthur Boot, a retired cordwainer wrote stupid letters to real, famous people, who, because they were famous, took the letters seriously and consequently wrote serious and, therefore, stupid replies. Below are a few examples:

The Arthur Boot Letters

14 Surbastapol Gardens
Surbiton
Surrey

Dear Pope

My wife and I will be passing close to Rome this summer and
wondered if it would be possible for us to stop off and be
presented to you? It is on account of the Catholics that we
live next door to having seventeen children, damage to the
roses, Dinky toys in the Flymo, and sun obscured at anything
but midday by miles of nappies, etc.

My wife and I would like to pop in and have an informal
chat, if at all possible with you and your wife, vis-à-vis
this family. Although we are C of E we do not hold anything
against Catholics, e.g. Terry Wogan. Many of them are **good
people**. We would however, welcome the opportunity of talking
to you, vis-à-vis contraception, etc.

I mentioned it to Mr Casey next door. He said that he
and his wife practised the rhythm method, but my wife said
how does he do it and play the marimba at the same time? It
an old joke but it may not have reached Rome yet.

We'll be passing Rome in our Travelhome next May. T
enclosed pound note is for the black baby fund.

Yours, in anticipation

ARTHUR BOOT

90

Dear Mr Boot

Thank you for your letter. You can come to tea Wed. 21 May
4.30 in the afternoon. My wife she say she will get some
Typhoo and muffins in for as how you are English. She also
say her brother Ginaro he runs big milk bar in Newcastle on
Tyne. If you go past she say you ask him please if parcel of
Parma ham and pickled radish arrive at Christmas. We hear of
Mr Casey before. We send two of the boys round when he fail
to keep up payments on PAPAL INCENSE-POWERED OVA PREDICT
COMPUTER. Unfortunately, wrong citizen ends up under
Blackfriars Bridge. Ah well, c'est la vie, que sera sera,
etc. etc.

You can recognise our house very easy. Go cross St
Peter's Square till you see the lines of nappies, Dinky toys,
bits of Lego, armless action-popes etc., go through broken
fence past the rusty bike with the stabilizer balance wheels
and the broken sledge. Tell one of the nuns with guns and
they'll come and wake me and my wife from siesta. Until then,
ciao, arrivederci and nastrova.

14 Surbastapol Terrace
Surbiton
Surrey

Dear Mrs Thatcher

That fiver I sent you last week for your fund made me feel
ashamed afterwards when I saw you on television speaking out
so forcibly in support of all the things that make Britain
great. For example, schools, National Health surcharge on
dentures and glasses, Henley Regatta, muffins, Devon cream
teas and the right of people in the north of England to be
unemployed. How little that five pound seemed afterwards,
consequently I am enclosing another five pounds towards your
slush funds. I would like you to use it particularly to do
with anything, vis-à-vis anti-Scargill or unions, or anything
of that ilk.

Who do these people think they are? That's what I want
to know.

Yours, with full support.

ARTHUR BOOT

PS Is your husband really such a wally?

10 Downing Street

Dear Mr Boot

Thank you for your letter of support and the five pound note.
       I agree whole-heartedly that at a time when so many of
our OAPs are being threatened by bully-boy tactics, miners
butting policemen's truncheons and hitting our brave
policemen's boots with their groins, etc., that any right-
thinking Englishman or woman who values the old values, the
Victorian values that made our country great, at a time when
it was indeed great, and who want to return to those values,
are going to support any party that stands up for the people
who support the things that it supports. You know, I remember
how when I was a girl in my father's grocer's shop in
Grantham, a pound of sugar could be wrapped in little blue
bags. We don't have those little blue bags anymore and I
think that the passing of those little blue bags represents
more than just the passing of those little blue bags, it
represents the passing of all the things that we in Britain
hold dear and to which you referred so ably in your letter.
       Thank you once again for the five pound note, and in
answer to your question - yes.

Another sort of book you could write if you wanted to make a fortune from writing books is a book of lists. It doesn't matter what sort of list, any will do. People for some reason, God only knows why but I'm one of them myself, cannot resist buying books of lists. You could make a book of lists nobody could prove or disprove, for example the world's ten most useless things.

THE WORLD'S TEN MOST USELESS THINGS

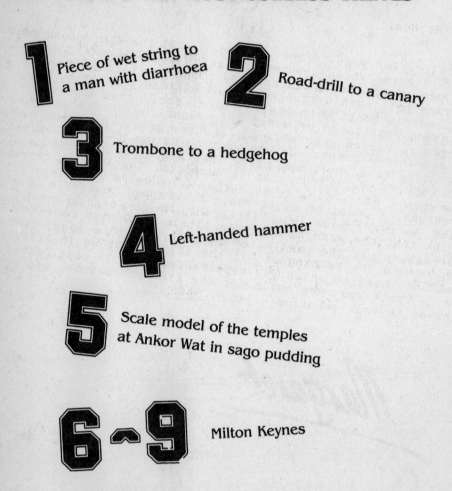

1 Piece of wet string to a man with diarrhoea

2 Road-drill to a canary

3 Trombone to a hedgehog

4 Left-handed hammer

5 Scale model of the temples at Ankor Wat in sago pudding

6-9 Milton Keynes

10 The architect who designed Milton Keynes

Another list you could include in your book of useless lists could be:

THE TEN LEAST-VISITED TOURIST TRAPS

1 Scunthorpe Floral Clock

2 The grave of the poet Arthur Trump*

3 Barnsley Lighthouse and Maritime Museum

4 The collection of bed-pans at Lock Jaw Hall

5 Grimsby Museum of Inkwells and Dildos

6 The White Horse of Eccles

7 Milton Keynes New Town

8 Milton Keynes Museum of strya-foam cups, crochetted poodle-shaped toilet-roll holders and brass tubular glass lamps with globules of oil that float up and down inside them when they are switched on.

9 Wolverhampton town trail

10 The house of Eric Doomesby, caretaker of St Scropulous School

*Arthur Trump (1810-1902), lesser known English poet who wrote such lines as: ▬▬ ▬

> *'I think that I have never seen a tree,*
> *A tree that is not almost all over green'.*

He was shot dead in a duel after he had insulted an Armenian oyster-opener in a bar near Wapping Old Stairs. He might have survived had he brought a gun instead of a sword. Arthur Trump also wrote:

> *'I wandered as isolated as smoke,*
> *And saw a lot of yellow flowers'*

Not many of his poems are remembered with either any great detail or affection.

You could also make a fortune from books by writing a book that showed you how you could make place names sound like other things. A famous example of such a book is The World According To Barf by Murray Christmas.

SCUNTHORPE: A scunthorpe is a small whitlow that grows on a bank teller's finger and means that he can't count notes above a certain denomination.

SHROEBURYNESS: Shroeburyness is the art of dancing in hot soup.

PADSTOW: A padstow is an off-centre hole in a long-playing record.

WALTON: A man who has sexual relationships with garden gnomes.

SEDBURGH: A sedburgh is a hard callow on the inside of the knees caused by riding a bicycle without a saddle.

PENGE: Penge is the noise a guillemot makes when it's mating.

CHIPPING NORTON: A chipping norton was a Cartesian monk responsible for grinding the bromide pellets into the tea urn.

Another book guaranteed to make you as rich as creosote is any book at all about the Royal Family. Because any book about the Royals is guaranteed to sell like chaud patisseries as they say in Chernonceaux. For example, you could do a book on:

PRINCE CHARLES'S COLLECTION OF POLO STICKS

ROYAL BABIES THROUGH THE YEARS

INTERESTING HABITS OF THE ROYAL CORGIS

EVEN MORE INTERESTING HABITS OF THE ROYAL ART ADVISORS

THE BOOK OF THE ROYAL HONEYMOON

THE BOOK OF THE ROYAL FIRST TIFF

Another sort of book that could be guaranteed to make you immense amounts of money is any book about animals, either a Book of British Dogs, Dead British Dogs, Famous British Dogs Belonging to Famous British People, or any book about little cuddly animals, such as rabbits, squirrels, field-mice or moles. So after Watership Down and Duncton Wood you could write a story of a life and death struggle in the underground kingdom of the worms. After rabbits and moles, why not? And you could even call your book Dungley Dell.

Snargla paused. In the warm damp dark he was alone. He pushed his head forward slightly. 'I want to make ploot,' he thought. He made ploot. 'It's my tunnel,' he thought, 'let the others worry if my ploot annoys them.' He moved his middle forward and plooted again. The ploot lingered in the tunnel. The tunnel walls trembled.

Gogs were moving on the hard sky of his world. Snargla shortened like a pink and white concertina. Two of his brothers had been taken by gogs and impaled on wire to be drowned on the ends of a line. One of his cousins had ended up in the stomach of a fish. The people of the Margla hated the gogs and magogs and rejoiced whenever they found a dead one buried in the Underbeing. Snargla heard noises behind him. It was Skitta and Skoorglie, two of the younger worms in the Underbeing. Skitta shivered violently.

'Did you just make a ploot?' asked Snargla.

'No it was you,' said Skitta.

Skitta went into one of his mystic trances. He spoke in a strange, faraway voice. 'I see whiteness whiter than the roof of the world above the world. I see many gogs and magogs. I see many sky-walkers with curved mouths coming very early. We must leave this place.'

'Pnish off!' said Skoorglie.

'What a loaf of pleat,' said Skandal The Brave, who had just arrived down the tunnel. 'What is there to be afraid of here? You're off your crust!' At that moment, from the world above the blade of a spade descended, neatly slicing Skandal The Brave in two. 'We're off,' said both ends of him as he crawled off in opposite directions.

Then again, of course, you could write a book about sex, perhaps a book that gives you advice about sex. You don't necessarily need to know much about it, since you can get much of your information from reading other books about it. Your book about sex could include, for example, Things You Should Never Say While Making Love.

WOMEN:

'There's a fly on the light-bulb.'

'Why do men have hairs in their ears?'

MEN:

'Shall I take my socks off?'

'That's never happened before.'

'I can't breathe if I do that.'

'Did you embroider this pillow yourself?'

Another way of making a lot of money from writing books is by writing parodies. Parodies are only really funny when they are written in the style of the original but contain some sort of a quirk. For example, you could rewrite The Wind In The Willows as though the action took place, not on the banks of the Thames near the green leafy swards of Reading (pre-silicone valley of course), but instead at Golders Green, or Cheetham Hill, or perhaps in Leeds.

THE WIND IN THE MATZOS

Mole had just finished dusting the shop. Dusting, how he hated dusting. Oy vey, if it wasn't enough that he had the cloth to buy and three pairs of trousers for Ruben waiting for alteration, now he had the shop to dust and the windows to clean.

'That!' to the cleaning he told himself. And he threw down the duster. 'I'm going outside.'

He struggled and buggled and waved his paws about as though he was selling and buying a million yards of cloth and POP! - he was out.

He blinked in the sunlight.

A fat rabbi went hopping past.

'Good morning, Rabbi,' said Mole.

'And to you too,' said the rabbi, hopping into the distance, 'Mazel Tov I wish.'

The mole had never smelt the air so fresh before. He wandered all day across the leafy meadows, gurgling-streams, through fields, lanes, all the places he'd never even been to before. 'This is the life for me,' he thought. Forget all the cutting and the schlepping and the tacking and the little treadle machine. Today the sun was shining and today Mole would have a holiday. Suddenly he was at the river. The river ran broad as another land, stretching from bank to bank. Mole stared at the river speechlessly, his tiny eyes opened wide, glinting like little black press-studs in the afternoon sunlight.

Below him a head popped out. 'All day you're going to stand there with your tongue hanging out - ain't you never seen a river before?'

'Ratty!' cried Mole 'How are you?'

'How am I? How am I, you ask? Six months he hasn't seen me and how am I, he asks. Ach, I'm all right. The children never come to see me, business is terrible, the roof is letting water in and tradesmen, can you find them? The woods are full of weazles, ferretts and schwarzers with transitor radios on their shoulders. It isn't safe for a rat to go out at nights nowadays. Last week alone three old otters coming back from the post office, their pension books they had taken off them. It isn't safe for a person to walk about nowadays. But you, you ask how am I? I'll tell you how I am - terrible. I'd go and live with the children, but can you impose? The eldest, a nice place he's got, a nice little hole behind the reception desk in a doctor's group practice. Nice classy place. The youngest, he's with a dentist, I wanted he should go with a doctor but he had his own mind. He's always been a strong-minded boy. What can you do? The daughter, you know the daughter. You know who she married? A caterer. Do I need to say anymore? So what do I do, can I impose, can I go and live with them? They've got their own lives to lead. Anyway, for why am I standing here all day talking to you? Come inside have a drink, sit. So? It's going to kill you?'

But I really think if you want to write a book you should start right at the top and write a novel. You don't know anything about it? Listen, if Jeffrey Archer can get away with it, so can you.

All you need is a good beginning,
'Once you've got them reading, you're away,' said George Bernard Shaw.

Below are several beginnings, you can have them free gratis and for nothing. Finish the novel, send it off and Mazel Tov.

JOURNEY INTO SPICE - A SEXUAL ODYSSEY

The moons of Erotica hung low over her southern horizon, casting a purple sheen on the eight-headed snargs that were unloading the giant transporter crash-landed in the centre of the humid yellow forest.

'Faster, you octogoons!' yelled Krang, the eighteen-foot tall Tzurgk warrior, his sinewy muscles rippling beneath his star-blasted skin.

From the shadows, Queen Labia of Erotica watched dully, almost bored by it all, her handmaidens fanning her with the fronds of the lilac zgonye plant, a famed aphrodisiac. Her nostrils flared a little. She lifted her little finger. 'Libido,' she summoned a squat fanged dwarf, 'fetch me that warrior.'

SUNDAY NIGHT AND MONDAY MORNING

Gleeson sat up in the gutter and spat some bits of teeth out. He tried to count with a swollen tongue. The first four seemed to have gone from the top and one or two from the bottom. It hadn't been a good idea to pinch the bride's bum like that, not when her brothers were watching.

He moved his hand around inside his shirt.

It didn't feel as though anything was broken, but something certainly felt sore.

He pushed himself up and moved gently down the street.

This was no way, he thought to himself, for a Bishop of the Holy Roman Catholic Church to be carrying on.

THE RAIDERS OF DRY GULCH CANYON OR TROUBLE AT THE LAZY Z

Shouting 'Yippee' and 'Gridleploop', Kit Carbuncle threw his leg over his faithful Palomino, inadvertently catching his wedding tackle on the pommel of his saddle. His eyes watered as he rode stiff-backed and watchful towards the Golden Rivet Saloon, conscious of the many pairs of eyes fixed on his back. A searing pain travelled through his loins like ink on a blotter as he reached for his six gun, only to find in his holster a stick of rock with the message, 'a present from Hanging Gulch, Colorado', along its length.

STAR WRECKS

Flash Ramsbottom adjusted the megatron, anti-matter boosters and set the space yacht spinning past the huge asteroid that was zooming towards them.

The space yacht, Bellerophon, rocked crazily as a hail of meteorite dust spattered against her hull.

'By gum, some speed, eh Digby?' he cried through clenched teeth.

'By 'eck, I wish Malcolm was here,' answered Digby, who was doing macrame by the pale light of the positron screen.

'Trust me to crew with a gay Yorkshireman,' thought Flash, as the yacht zoomed on at the speed of doubt.

SCARBOROUGH ROCK

Mulligan knew he was going to die the minute he stepped off the train in Scarborough. It wasn't just the safe that fell from the fourteenth storey of the Royal Hotel and narrowly missing him, or the fourteen geriatrics in wheelchairs that chased him to the foot of the lifeboat steps where he escaped by climbing over the gypsy palm-reader's stall. It wasn't even the three old ladies that fell from the bridge above Happy Valley, two of them landing in the rockery at his side, the third completely demolishing the rock, candy floss and bingo stall in front of him. It was the ticking toffee-apple that blew up when he threw it away and took with it a deckchair attendant and seven old ladies that finally clinched it for him. It was too much for it to be a coincidence.

TIME WALK

Silas K. Frogbottom knew he was in Hell the third time he opened the door to a room and found that he was back again in Westcliffe-on-Sea. Three times he had escaped, once to a motorway services on the M1, once to a motel on the Norfolk Broads and now to a police station in Glasgow Central, where on opening the door of the gents toilets he had found himself back again in the same damp room in Sunny Vistas, Westcliffe-on-Sea, looking out at the mud and the refineries of the Isle of Sheppey. There was no escape.

If you can draw a little, or if you can draw not at all, then the world is looking for you, and for books like A Thousand And One Uses Of A Dead Hedgehog.

A Thoasand and One Uses Of a Dead Hedgehog

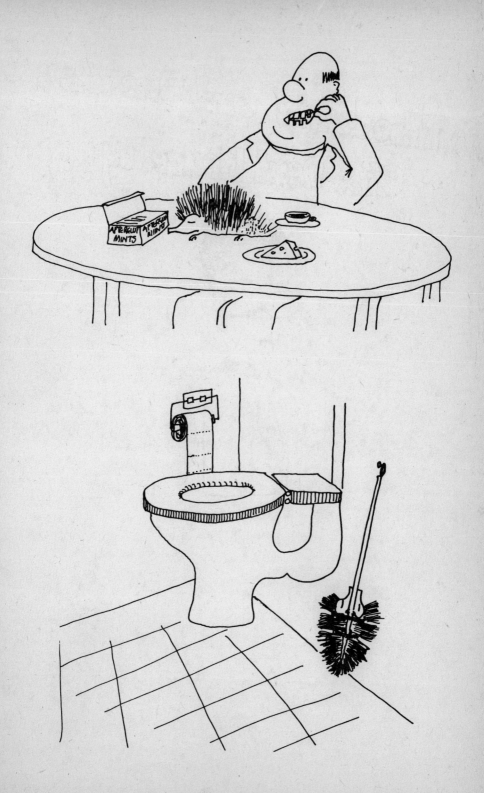

A Thoasand and One Uses Of a Dead Hedgehog

1st   *Penguin: Did you know they named a chocolate biscuit after us?*

2nd *Penguin: What? Syd and Mabel?*

* * * * * *

Have you ever felt you were better than people think you to be?
Have you ever felt that you knew exactly what this country needs?
Have you ever felt that with the right connections you could get on in the world?
Are you a little shit?
Then grow a small toothbrush moustache, comb your hair across your forehead and -
Join the Young Conservatives - now!

* * * * * *

Booby Trap

Mazeltov Cocktail

'We will defend to the death the
rights of all free peoples
everywhere to die for whatever we
think fit at the time, particularly if
they are poor, black or
Communists. Was that all right
Nancy? Did I say it right? Did I
get the emphasis in the right
place?'

On hearing the First Cuckoo in Spring